PATHWAYTO PROSPERITY

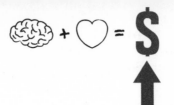

PATHWAY TO PROSPERITY

THE 12 STEPS TO FINANCIAL FREEDOM

PAT MESITI

Wrightbooks

First published in 2013 by Wrightbooks
an imprint of John Wiley & Sons Australia, Ltd
42 McDougall St, Milton Qld 4064

Office also in Melbourne

Typeset in 10.5/12.5 pt ITC Giovanni Std

© Pat Mesiti 2013

The moral rights of the author have been asserted

National Library of Australia Cataloguing-in-Publication entry:

Author:	Mesiti, Pat.
Title:	Pathway to prosperity: the 12 steps to financial freedom / Pat Mesiti.
ISBN:	9781118523995 (pbk.)
Subjects:	Finance, Personal.
	Wealth.
Dewey Number:	332.024

Internal design by Peter Reardon, pipelinedesign.com.au

Cover design by saso content & design

Author photo: Dennis Iezzi

Printed in China by Printplus Limited

10 9 8 7 6 5 4 3 2 1

Disclaimer
The material in this publication is of the nature of general comment only, and does not represent professional advice. It is not intended to provide specific guidance for particular circumstances and it should not be relied on as the basis for any decision to take action or not take action on any matter which it covers. Readers should obtain professional advice where appropriate, before making any such decision. To the maximum extent permitted by law, the author and publisher disclaim all responsibility and liability to any person, arising directly or indirectly from any person taking or not taking action based on the information in this publication.

*To my daughter Sophia Grace Mesiti,
our joy bringer.*

Contents

About the author

$$$$$

Pat is a highly effective communicator and income acceleration coach. His passion is to equip and empower individuals and businesses to experience growth and prosperity to their full potential. He is an expert in shifting mindsets and building bigger people to produce results.

Pat has spoken at some of the largest conferences around the world, and his books and materials have sold over two million copies. Having built some of Australia's largest people–driven organisations, Pat understands the power of harnessing people's potential.

Pat Mesiti's enthusiasm combined with his great sense of humour gives him the ability to move an audience into action as well as give them practical resources to help them achieve their goals. He is a gifted communicator and adds tremendous value to the lives he touches. Pat is dynamic, entertaining and unforgettable!

Acknowledgements

Thank you to Kirstie Wood for always being there to type up my messes. A big thank you to Steven Slaven Spehar for checking the manuscript in the early days and giving me great insights. To Mark Badham for transcribing and translating my thoughts. To my editor Jem Bates—you are absolutely brilliant. To everyone in the Mesiti team for your tireless hard work. And thank you to my beautiful wife Andrea, who is selfless.

Introduction

Are you where you want to be?

I have a goal to create 10 000 millionaires in my lifetime. That's why I run special events every year. That's why I travel the world speaking to men and women who hunger for financial success. That's why I've written this book. You see, I want *you* to become wealthy and prosperous, and I believe you can.

The word *prosperity* comes from the Latin *prosperare*, which means to *prosper, thrive* or *flourish*. I love those words! And I know you do too. After all, that's why you picked up this book. Unfortunately, most people can't honestly use these words to describe their life. So many of us aspire to prosperity, but our reality is quite different. We want to be financially secure, but we're struggling to get there. The purpose of this book is to help you get from where you are now to where you want to be. I want to show you how to live your life by design, not by default.

Some 98 per cent of people spend their lives working hard, only to end up with fewer financial resources than they had planned. Most would confess that financially their life did not turn out the way they had hoped it would. In *Million Dollar Habits*, speaker and author Robert Ringer wrote: 'The world is saturated with intelligent, highly educated, extraordinarily skilled people who experience ongoing frustration because of their lack of success. Millions of others spend their lives working hard, long hours only to die broke.' In 2010 the National Bureau of Economic Research found that nearly

50 per cent of Americans would be unable to come up with $2000 in 30 days if an emergency arose. That means half the country is living one pay cheque away from financial collapse.

There is often a tension between where we want to end up in life and the path we choose to get there. We fail to see that good intentions are never enough. We need to understand why, despite our good intentions, we may have ended up at the wrong financial destination. One reason is that we are surrounded by people who are moving in the wrong direction *with us*. In recent years in Australia, New Zealand, the US and the UK, for example, many people made the same bad decisions that led to too much debt: they bought overpriced houses they could not afford while they did not have enough savings in the bank. When everyone around us is doing the same thing we're doing, it's easy to deceive ourselves into thinking it will work out. And when we end up where those poor decisions take us, we're confused about how we got there.

Over the years I've talked to many individuals and couples with financial problems who assure me they are close to a solution — a fix here or an adjustment there. But just as there is no easy fix when you accidentally wind up a hundred miles from where you want to be on a road trip, there is no quick fix when you wake up to the reality that you are far away from where you want to be financially.

Some years ago I was in Los Angeles and decided to drive myself to the airport. My hosts had given me some simple directions and a hand-drawn, step-by-step map, so I climbed into the rental car, grabbed the wheel and took off. My objective was to negotiate a labyrinth of interconnected freeways in a foreign city, yet I was so confident I decided to take a shortcut. Instead of getting onto Interstate 405, I decided to take another freeway that I thought would get me to the airport a lot quicker.

It wasn't long before it dawned on me that I had taken a wrong turn, but I didn't stop. I just kept driving. An hour later

I found myself in what looked like one of the most rundown city neighbourhoods in America. Here I was, a budding young preacher travelling the globe, selling my message of good news, driving a rental car loaded with suitcases and t-shirts, and I had no idea where I was. I began to get nervous, and the more wrong turns I took, the more anxious I became. Worse still, it was dark outside and I could no longer see the street signs.

As I turned into a small street I noticed a light outside a van selling burgers. By now I was ready to ask for directions, so I pulled up next to the burger stand and got out of the car. As I began to ask for directions I suddenly found myself surrounded by four young men. 'What are you doing around here?' one asked. 'This is not your place!'

Here I was in a dark street, in a foreign city, absolutely lost, accosted by four gang members. My knees started shaking and my mouth went dry. I knew I was in deep trouble, but all that came to mind was Crocodile Dundee. And in moments like that you don't think, you just act. So in a broad, true-blue Australian accent, I said, 'Oh, g'day fellas. I'm from Australia and I'm trying to find Los Angeles Airport. I'm totally lost!'

The mood changed in an instant. They stepped back and smiled. 'You're from Australia? You know Crocodile Dundee?'

'Yeah, I'm a neighbour,' I replied. 'I live just down the road from his place.'

'Man, we love that scene where he says, "That's not a knife — this is a knife!"'

'Yeah, in Australia we all carry knives like that.'

We were instant friends. Those boys ended up giving me directions to get back on track. The difference was that this time I listened.

Now I want to give you some directions too, so listen up. The first thing you've got to do is recognise where you are right now financially. Be very honest with yourself (after all, this is just between you and me). Don't let another day go by in which you ignore the real situation you are in. Once you've given it some attention, ask yourself, did you plan to arrive where you are today or did you arrive here by accident? In other words, are you where you are by design or by default?

If you're massively in debt, tied to a business or job you don't like or living in a home in a suburb that's not ideal, then my guess is you're not there by design. But if you're there by default, I don't want you to worry too much... because you're not alone. You're living in a society full of people just like you.

Now it's my turn to be very honest with you: I'm here to tell you that you are where you are today largely because of the steps you took along the way. It's no good placing the blame on your upbringing, your background, your education, your accountant or the government. *You* are responsible for your current financial situation. But here's the upside: *you* can do something about it. You can get out of your current financial surroundings. You can reduce your debt, increase your worth, make wiser investments... and even give away a lot more than you do now. And I want to help you get there.

Do you remember that great song by the band Talking Heads called 'We're on a Road to Nowhere'? You may feel like that sometimes. Or maybe you feel you're on a carousel and don't know how to get off. I have some good news for you: you *can* change the path you're on. Your destination — your destiny — is in your hands. It's up to you where you end up — with your finances, your business or career, your relationships and even your health. If you follow the right pathways you will prosper in all these areas. You just need to ask for directions, take advice and stick to the right roads. And if you find you are on the wrong pathway, you can get off again and find the right one. It's your choice. It's not too late to jump onto the path that leads to financial success.

If there's one thing you don't need in your world it's another solution, another quick fix, another get-rich-quick scheme. Some of us think, *Oh if I could just get connected on the internet*

it would be the answer to my financial problems. Or, I'll buy and sell a few properties, and then I'll be able to retire in a few years. Wrong! Most likely you'll make the kinds of decisions you've always made and end up financially worse off. Why? Because you are looking for solutions. This book is about directions, not solutions. If you want to get from where you are to where you want to be financially, the answer is not in a solution. The answer is getting the right directions to steer you onto the right pathways to financial freedom. Certain pathways will surely lead to financial rewards; others will guarantee your financial ruin. Pathways are predictable like that.

A lot of people tell me they want to 'make it' financially. 'I want to make it in business,' they say. 'I want to make it in property!' 'I want to make it in the stock market!' Well, I don't agree. I don't want you to *make* it. I want you to *build* it. There is a huge difference between making it and building it. In the 30+ years I've been helping people create prosperity, I've seen many people make it and then lose it. Making money is not as important as building it. I want to teach you how to build your wealth so that it sustains you for many years to come. I want to increase your capacity to earn money over time. I want you to enjoy life, to prosper and flourish long term, to experience all the good things life has to offer, to taste what it's like to live a life of abundance and increase.

Why am I encouraging you to build a life of prosperity? Because I've learned that money is good and that there's enough of it on this Earth for everyone. I want to acquire all I can, give all I can and save all I can. And I am committed to the financial success of others, including you. In fact, I hope you will become one of my 10 000 millionaires. Will you join me on the pathway to prosperity?

Chapter 1

What path are you on?
The pathway to your prosperity

Late one night, many years ago, I received a phone call that my father had collapsed. We knew he had been suffering from cancer, but we weren't yet aware of how far the cancer had spread through his body. I hung up the phone, jumped in the car and sped off towards his home. I'd had a very busy day, and now I was on my way to see my father for what might be the last time. In my frantic state, I made an impulsive decision to try a new route. Between my father's home and mine a new housing estate had sprung up. I had never driven through the area, but that night (it was long before the days of car navigation systems) I decided to navigate my way through the maze of new streets to try to save time.

Now, those who know me well know I don't have a strong sense of geographical direction at the best of times (a shortcoming already illustrated in the introduction), but that night I was desperate to get to my father as quickly as possible. As I ventured into the new suburb I became aware of three problems: first, the street lights had not been switched on; second, some of the street signs had not yet been erected; and third, there was no moonlight. It was pitch black outside, but now I was committed. My journey had its own momentum and, a typical man, I was incapable of turning back or stopping to ask for directions.

Five minutes later I knew I was lost and for the first time I felt a wave of panic sweep over me. The more I panicked, the more lost I became, and the more I was lost, the more distressed and desperate I became. Now I couldn't remember how to get back and I had no idea how to move forward in the right direction. I was lost in the dark… and my father was dying.

Getting utterly lost like that is a horrible experience, but getting lost financially has far greater implications. Have you arrived at a financial destination you hadn't planned for? Is it less rewarding than you had expected? Have you found yourself in a financial rut that you can't see any way out of? Like me that night, you may have found yourself lost (financially, I mean) with no signs to guide you back on course.

I did eventually find my father's house, and I got to talk to him before he passed away a few weeks later. Being lost — geographically or financially — is something we have all experienced. In this book I want to show you how to find your way out of the financial fog. I want to show you how to get from where you are now financially to where you need to be — to show you how to build wealth. My aim is to equip you with some incredible tools that will help you build a life that is financially rewarding for you, your family, your friends and your community.

Recently I read a book that changed my life. It's called *The Principle of the Path* and in it author Andy Stanley describes a unifying principle that governs what happens in every area of our lives, including our finances. Let me unravel this principle a little more.

Whether you know it or not, you are on a path heading somewhere in life. Some paths lead to good destinations; others lead to less desirable places. Your destination is determined by the decisions you make throughout your life. It has nothing to do with your level of intelligence, education, goals or even wealth. In other words, it doesn't matter how educated or smart you are, or how connected you are when you start out — if you're on the wrong path you'll end up at the wrong place. The only way to get to your desired destination is to pick the right path.

With the right information, pathways to wealth can be predictable. Most of our financial challenges are the result of bad advice. That's why it's critical that we ask for directions from the right people.

How do I start for the Emerald City?

Remember *The Wizard of Oz*? For those of you who are too young to have seen the movie or read the book, let me summarise the story, because there's a life-changing lesson in that old classic. Dorothy has been swept into a strange world by a storm and she sets out to find her way home. First she meets Glinda, the good witch of the north. Glinda tells her she must seek advice from the great wizard of Oz, who lives in the Emerald City. Dorothy asks: 'But how do I start for the Emerald City?' It's a simple question that

If you're on the wrong path you'll end up at the wrong place.

we should all ask when we start out on our financial journey. I'm not saying we should all head for the Emerald City, of course. But the Emerald City can symbolise our financial destinations, and the sooner we ask the right questions, the sooner we will begin to make progress.

'How do I start out to have my car paid off in three years?'

'How do I start out to save enough money to pay for my children's education?'

'How do I start out to own three homes in 10 years?'

'How do I start out to have enough money to retire at age 60?'

And Glinda's famous answer applies to all of us seeking to know how to get from where we are to a place of financial success. She tells Dorothy: 'It's always best to start at the beginning—and all you do is follow the yellow brick road.'

Now, like any journey in life, Dorothy encounters a few obstacles that could have knocked her off course and even stopped her progress, but she doesn't get sidetracked or lost. What's her secret? She sticks strictly to the path. She takes one step at a time, following that yellow brick road. Eventually she finds herself in the Emerald City simply because that's where the yellow brick road led, and that was the path *she chose*.

The origin of the path

The principle of the path is not a new idea—it's as old as humanity, cutting across time, religion and culture. As the late Jim Rohn would have said, beware of the man who tries to sell you a new antique. Sometimes, though, the familiar can be missed, forgotten in the rush. Over the years I have seen the path lead a lot of people to great financial, emotional and personal rewards. At the same time, I have seen the principle violated, ignored or mishandled with sometimes devastating consequences. When I ran a drug rehabilitation centre in Sydney I worked with young men who had chosen a path whose destination was predictable to everyone except the person in the middle of it. We never deliberately choose to follow a destructive path. Most of life's personal as well as financial disasters are a result of poor decision making based on quite subtle influences. You sow a thought, you reap an act; you sow an act, you reap a habit; you sow a habit, you form a destiny.

Let me offer an illustration. A young man who desperately seeks the approval of his friends jumps at the chance to go out partying with them. One of his older buddies passes around a joint. At first he is shocked, then there's the adrenalin rush and he thinks, 'Hey, all my friends are doing it,' and once never hurt anyone, did it? So he takes his first step. As time goes by the occasional puff isn't enough. He's rolling joints, and his friends don't discourage it—in fact, they think it's pretty cool and he's feeling more accepted. Then they start to go to all-night dance parties where someone offers him a pill to keep him feeling high all night. Of course, he has no idea what's in it or who made it. That's his second step. He has no job now, and his behaviour is starting to form a pattern. When he's not taking dope, depression kicks in and he feels like no-one understands him. His parents just don't get him, his father is always picking on him and then his girlfriend dumps him. Someone suggests he try shooting up, because it feels great and you can just escape all the hassles of life for a while. Soon he's injecting heroin, and before you know it he's caught breaking and entering. Now he's an addict facing a prison sentence.

Let me give you another illustration. He's a middle-aged man and a bit of a workaholic. At home the zing has gone out of his marriage, and the more hostile the relationship becomes, the more he retreats into work. It's just as well he earns a good salary, because they keep needing new stuff — a new car, a bigger home as the kids grow up and need more room to play (they can't just go to the park or the beach). Starved of intimacy at home, he starts to take more notice of a cute girl in the office, and she obviously likes him. The truth is, she can't help comparing him with her lazy bum of a boyfriend and thinking how nice it would be to be looked after the way this guy obviously looks after his family. So they find more excuses to be in each other's company and they text each other all the time…now you fill in the blanks. How many of you can recognise this path?

I'm not here as anyone's moral policeman, but let's apply the same principle to your financial life. You start off with a manageable home mortgage. Later you want something bigger, and you need new furniture because the old stuff doesn't quite work in the new house. Of course, like every soccer mum you need a four-wheel-drive big enough to fit five kids (even though you have only one), and you have to buy new clothes, even though you've hardly worn most of last year's. If your husband could just land that new job or if he was paid what he was really worth, you'd be able to afford these things — and, by the way, the new iPhone and iPad are coming out soon so of course you'll need those. Oh and our friends are going away for a three-day luxury weekend — I know it's a little expensive on top of our three weeks in the snow and the two weeks at the beach in the summer, but don't we deserve it?

Can you see the pattern here? When people with a Kmart income want to live a Gucci lifestyle, no wonder their path leads to financial ruin. None of these pleasures are wrong in themselves. If you can afford the new car and all the other stuff, go for it, but if you want to play now you have to understand that you'll end up paying for it for the rest of your life.

Our steps form a path in one direction

What steps have you taken that brought you to where you are today? The truth is that every financial decision you make is a step in a certain direction. Each decision you make is connected to the next and the next... Your decisions form a pattern that eventually connects you from A to B right through to Z. In time you can look back on your life or your business or your career and see how the decision dots connected to lead you to where you are now.

> Your decisions form a pattern that eventually connects you from A to B right through to Z.

It's funny how we can shake our heads over the patterns of behaviour we see in other people's lives yet we cannot see them in our own life! I'm sure you know people who seem to have it all together and you've wondered how they did it, because you don't know them well enough to see the right decisions — which are often the tough decisions — they made along the way. That's the truth of it: these people made more right decisions than others.

Recently I was watching the Wallabies play the All Blacks in a rugby match. From high up in the stadium, I could look down on the field and see all the players in their respective positions as the match unfolded. During critical stages in the game I even saw try-scoring opportunities forming before the players themselves would have seen them. That's the advantage of an elevated view: you can see the steps taken and the momentum building in a certain direction much better than you can at ground level. But I found it frustrating to watch because there was nothing I could do about it.

As parents, we look at patterns of behaviour in young people and we try to warn them of the outcomes of poor decisions. They tell us they plan to go out and enjoy a couple of drinks. In the madness of the moment they decide to have another one, and another one. Then they get introduced to a new crowd and the rounds of drinks start again. Sooner or later drugs may be passed around too. Combine that with the wrong crowd and accidents start to happen. From a helicopter view you can see the steps taken that lead to that outcome, but at ground level it's harder to connect the dots.

I have a friend whose brothers tried to help him in business, but he ended up getting thrown out of the family firm. His father tried to set him up in another business, but it went broke. So he started his own business, but he often turned up late and his customers complained about the work. When his parents passed away they left him and his siblings an inheritance. Today he doesn't own a home, he doesn't own any shares, and he has very little superannuation for his retirement. So what did he do with the money his parents left him? He bought a brand-new V8 sports car with all the options. Did he think that that one step could lead to his being being broke for the rest of his life? Did he think to invest, to save? No, he drove out with a new, cripplingly expensive car but with the same broke mindset he started with. Can you see a pattern here? The decisions he made showed the pathway he was on...but he himself couldn't see it. He may have had the best intentions. He may have had a wonderful dream of how his life would one day look, but there was something fundamentally missing.

Our direction determines our destination

Most bad financial decisions are the result of bad advice rather than bad or naive intentions, but naive intentions plus bad advice, I have discovered, equals financial disaster. I have found, too, that *no* advice also leads to financial disaster.

Good advice coupled with good intentions from someone who knows what they are doing, on the other hand, can lead you to a prosperous life. It's not our intentions that determine our destination, it's our direction. We can have the best of intentions in our business pursuits, but that won't determine the outcome. The direction in which you are currently travelling will determine where you end up in every area of your life. You can't hop into your car and drive west and expect to end up in the east.

It's not your prayers, your morality, your outstanding character, your intellect or your education that will determine your financial destination. It's the steps you take each day. If you get suckered by the lures of zero per cent financing, no deposit needed and no payments for 12 months, then you're on a one-way track to eventual financial hardship.

Most of us can think of prominent sports stars who, with all the money and potential in the world, ended up in financial ruin. According to *Sports Illustrated*, almost 80 per cent of US National Football League players find themselves bankrupt or in financial difficulty within two years of their retirement, and 60 per cent of former National Basketball Association players end up broke within five years of retirement.

Remember Scottie Pippen, the Chicago Bulls basketball player known to be Michael Jordan's sidekick? He lost $120 million in career earnings. He blew $27 million on bad investments and spent $4.3 million on a Gulfstream II corporate jet! According to his 2006 autobiography, two-time PGA golf champion John Daly gambled away between $50 million and $60 million in career earnings. Daly once lost $1.65 million in five hours playing the slot machines at a casino. Later he blew $1.2 million in two hours and 30 minutes at a Las Vegas casino. Perhaps the worst offender of them all, boxer Mike Tyson, squandered a fortune estimated at between $350 million and $400 million. 'Iron' Mike spent more than $4.5 million on cars alone, including half a million on a 420-horsepower Bentley Continental SC with lamb's wool rugs, a phone and a removable glass roof. He filed for bankruptcy in 2003.

'I would never waste my hard-earned money that way!' I hear you say. I hope you're right, but the truth is we all lean too hard on our intentions rather than setting out in the right direction. I've heard all the excuses: 'I meant to do the right thing!'... 'I meant to be a great provider for my family!'... 'I didn't mean to invest my money in the stock market and lose it!' Well of course not! But the fact is that many of us do! What prompts us to take such gambles? Is it greed? Is it that we're in too much of a hurry?

Someone I know recently lost $250 000 on the stock market trying to make money fast. Here is the tragedy: it wasn't even his money. His parents had borrowed the money for another project, but he convinced them that this was a sure bet, that he couldn't lose, that it was a guaranteed investment — and he lost it all! Should he have invested in the stock market? Absolutely. How much should he have invested? As much as he could afford to lose. His intentions were honourable. He wanted to be financially free. But the steps he took put him on a path to ruin. And it's one thing to lose your own money, but you've got to be a complete jerk to lose someone else's!

Do not believe the popular but life-destroying notion that if your intentions are good and your heart is in the right place, if you do your best and try your hardest, you are going to end up achieving your dreams. Let me give it to you straight: that's a pack of lies! I wish it were true, but it simply isn't. Your direction, not your intentions, will determine your financial destination.

> Your direction, not your intentions, will determine your financial destination.

I know young couples who began their married life together determined to be financially free, yet they constantly leased new cars, ate out at expensive restaurants and bought the latest electronic gadgets — all for great reasons too — and then 10 or 20 years later they wonder why they haven't been able to save up enough money for a home deposit. They can't see the pattern, but you and I can.

Here's another principle of the path: we never really know *when* we started getting lost. If we knew exactly when we became lost, we would stop right there, turn around and go back to that point so we could get back on the right road. But we don't get lost on purpose. We never start any journey with the intention of getting lost.

The road we are on determines where we end up

The road we are on always determines where we end up, because we always end up where the road we have chosen takes us. If you have found yourself on a path that's leading you away from where you want to go, slow down. One of the bad habits people have is they rush through life making quick decisions on their finances. It's important that you stop rushing through life and learn to take smaller steps in the direction you want to go. I have learned that you can get anywhere you want to in life, as long as you are willing to stay on the right road and take small steps. Every time you take a small step in the right direction, you are extending a sequence of good steps. The more correct steps you take, the closer you are getting to your financial dream, and the more abundance you will experience in your life. Every small step, good or bad, contributes to a sequence, a pattern. Small missteps can eventually lead to chaotic financial situations.

People function better when there is order in their life. When you increase your capacity for order, such as getting up early in the morning to go to the gym, investing 10 per cent of your income in a savings account, even giving away 10 per cent every week, your small, ordered steps put you on a path towards financial strength.

You don't need a solution

Is it possible that there is a yellow brick road leading to financial freedom for every one of us? If so, we could stop looking for solutions to our financial problems and start searching instead for the right path, the right direction...and to recognise that when it comes to money, it's either *now* or it's too late. Solutions don't fix financial issues — a good direction does, coupled with the right advice and the right steps. Change direction, then get a solution. This is the first step in understanding the principle of the path, because solutions are for computers that don't work, or for receding hairlines, or for trouser legs that are too long (a common problem for me!). Solutions don't often fix people. Direction is what we most need.

When I look back at my own life, I can see patterns in my behaviour, decisions I made that led me in a certain direction financially. The steps I have taken have led me to where I am today. Here's what's amazing: if you had made the same decisions I made, you too would be where I am today. In the same way, if I had made the same financial decisions you made all your life, I would be where you are right now. You see, pathways are no respecters of people. Money does not know the difference between a priest and a pornographer. Your moral intentions mean nothing to money; it follows your direction and instructions. Someone with good intentions and bad direction will still end up in financial ruin.

Take a look back at your own life and try to see the pattern in the decisions you took that led you to where you are today financially. Some things happen to us that affect us financially but are out of our control. I understand that. But I'm sure you'll be able to see a sequence of steps all the same. The mistake most of us make is that at the time we make financial decisions we aren't aware how those decisions will lead us to another decision and then another. We aren't aware of all the connections that form a pathway or pattern.

We must always remember that an individual decision or event is not isolated — it's a step on a path, because everything is connected. I may not intend to get into debt by buying that new plasma TV or the new car, but the decision will affect me in other areas of my life. We must be aware of both the obvious and the subtle gaps between our lifestyle and what we can actually afford. Will my decisions give me what I really need? By asking yourself the right questions you can find the right answers. I have learned rather painfully that you cannot turn back the hands of time to remake a poor decision, and there are some dreams and fortunes that can't be had because you missed the opportunity, but you can make a better choice next time.

Whether you recognise it or not, you have been on a financial path your whole adult life. And you alone are responsible for placing yourself on that pathway. Today the choice is yours. You can continue travelling down the same pathway you're on or you can put yourself back on the right track. But before you can do that you have to know *where* it is you want to go. That's the subject of the next chapter.

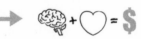

Take steps now in the right direction

Take a moment to look back at your life. Write down just a few of the major decisions you've made that have affected your financial situation today. It could be to put your overseas holiday on the credit card, or to buy your first home, or to lease or buy your partner's car, or to invest in the stock market. List the main ones here:

1 _____

2 _____

3 _____

Now identify a pattern in those decisions. Does it give you a picture of the pathway you've taken? Is the pattern clearer now? If not, take another look. This is a great starting point to making sure you find the right pathway for you.

Chapter 2

Where are you heading?
Know your destination

In the late 1960s a British teenager was struggling at school. No matter how hard he tried, his academic results were consistently dismal. While still at school, the 15 year old started two ventures, one growing Christmas trees and another raising budgerigars. Both failed financially. At the age of 16, he quit school and moved to London, where he began a student magazine. Against the odds, it was deemed a great success. At 20, he bought crates of cutout records from a discounter and sold them out of the boot of his car to retail outlets in London. This was the beginning of a record label that would become a worldwide music phenomenon. The company's first album sold more than five million copies. He signed the outrageous Sex Pistols when other record companies refused to touch them. He went on to sign up performers such as Roy Orbison, Genesis, Keith Richards, Janet Jackson and Culture Club.

In 1984 he decided to build an airline. Today the airline carries more than five million passengers a year, making it the eighth largest UK airline based on passenger numbers. Years later, in 1999, he launched a global mobile phone service provider, competing against giants such as Vodafone, Orange and AT&T. It too became a huge success.

He wasn't always successful in business, though. In 1994 he made a bid to run the National Lottery, promising to give all the profits to charity... and lost. He failed with a second bid five years later. In 1997 he took over part of Britain's ageing railway network. Despite the introduction of new trains, the network is still dogged by delays and service interruptions.

According to the *Forbes* 2011 list of billionaires, he is the fourth richest British citizen and the 254th richest person in the world. Besides his business interests, he is also an environmentalist, adventurer and philanthropist. His name, of course, is Sir Richard Branson and his business empire, consisting of more than 400 companies around the world, is the Virgin Group, whose net worth in 2008 was £5 billion.

So where are *you* heading? What's *your* dream? In the movie *Pretty Woman*, a man in the street asks us: 'What's your dream? Everybody comes to Hollywood got a dream. What's your dream?' Right now you may feel like you are a million miles from reaching your dream. Compared with people like Richard Branson, perhaps you feel like your life is going nowhere fast. Many of us feel this way at times. Maybe you feel like you didn't plan to be where you are financially. For you, life just happened. Forces outside of your control took over the financial direction of your life. But be honest: outside forces did not cause your money problems. The global financial crisis (GFC), which many people use as an excuse for their financial woes, did not cause your problems. The GFC revealed the financial problems you already had. A crisis simply reveals problems that already exist.

Take control of your financial future

How many times have you heard someone say, 'Don't worry, it'll work out in the end!' or 'We'll be fine — let's just not stress about our money situation'? They ended up with less money than they had hoped for, having relied more on luck than on a plan. If that's you, then I want to give you some hope. I want to show you how to take more control over your financial future. To start with, think about the three Cs: *clarity, consistency* and *coaching*. First, you must determine clearly what you want. Second, you must be consistent in your decisions and in your behaviour. Third, you need to get coaching from someone who can help you make money faster and better.

To build wealth into your life, here's the first key: *get a dream*. I'm not talking about a daydream. I mean a DREAM: a compelling picture of your future that will motivate you to move in that direction, a dream that drives you every day, even when you're down and outside forces seem to be conspiring against you. The truth is, sometimes we just haven't taken the time to think through what it is we actually want. We think we know, but we struggle to articulate it. This is a very basic starting point for developing our financial destination and our route to getting there. It's really not rocket science. Life is so simple — we go to university to mess it up!

So what do you want in life financially? Where do you want to live? What kind of home do you want to own? What kind of car do you want to drive? What amount of superannuation do you want when you retire? Now, don't go straight to 'I can't afford it!' or 'I couldn't get that!' Making up your mind is the first step. The rest is about time, getting the right advice, decision making, planning... and the right path to get you there. But if you don't know clearly *what* you want and *where* you want to be, how will you ever choose the right path?

What's your dream?

You need to know what you really, *really* want. If you don't make up your mind, your mind will make itself up, or others will decide your path for you. You don't want to get to the end of your life and wonder, *How did I get here? Why did I end up here?* Everyone ends up somewhere, whether they mean to or not. Today, through this book, you have the opportunity to make sure that you end up where you *want* to be, but you'll do so only by design and planning — prosperity is not an accident.

Too many people constantly look back on their lives. I have learned that your mind has a compartment called memory and another called imagination. Memory replays the past and keeps you contained by past experience, whereas imagination propels you towards your future and can create great wealth. Wealth comes out of your imagination, not out of your memory. Every new idea, product, event and speech comes out of imagination. Which compartment do you want to use more?

Someone once said, 'The poorest man is not without a cent, but without a dream.' You've got to have a dream. People who don't have a dream about their future don't know where they are heading. They don't know their destination. You've got to know where you want to end up, because when you know what you want, you can start to make plans.

> Wealth comes out of your imagination, not out of your memory.

Dreams are the catalyst for releasing extraordinary achievements and prosperity. In 1982, at the official opening of the newly completed Epcot Center at Disney World in Florida, one of the Disney executives turned to Walt Disney's widow and exclaimed, 'If only Walt could have seen this!'

'He did,' she replied. 'That's why it's here.'

The extent of your future prosperity is constrained only by the size of your dream today. So become a big dreamer. Characteristically, Donald Trump once said, 'You have to think anyway, so why not think big?' When launching Virgin Atlantic Airways, Richard Branson said his interest in life came from setting himself huge, apparently 'unachievable' challenges and trying to rise above them — dreaming big.

Does it cost us anything to dream bigger? Then why do we have such small dreams? Where did we learn that? It doesn't take much effort to dream big. Anyone can have a great dream. Do you have a big dream for your work or business? For your home and family? Here's why a big dream is important: whatever it is that you dream big, that's what will create your motivation and inspire you to stick to the right path.

The seed of your dream is a critical key to your prosperity. James Allen, author of *As a Man Thinketh*, wrote, 'Dreams are the seedlings of reality.' There is nothing more powerful than a dream that is watered and fed over time.

Successful people dream

Author and businessman Harvey Mackay said, 'Show me someone who doesn't dream about the future and I'll show you someone who doesn't know where he or she is going.' After studying high achievers extensively, Harvard psychologist David McClelland concluded that successful people possess one common characteristic: they fantasise incessantly about how to achieve their goals.

'We grow great by dreams,' said US president Woodrow Wilson. 'All great people are dreamers. They see things in the soft haze of a spring day or in the red fire of a long winter's evening. Some of us let these dreams die, but others nourish and protect them, nurse them through the bad days until they bring them to the sunshine and light that comes always to those who sincerely hope that their dreams will come true.'

> Your dream is one of your most powerful assets.

Your dream is one of your most powerful assets. In many cases, it's more powerful than your present reality. A dream is the imaginary, intangible vision you use to create a tangible future. Your reality is your present situation, but your present is only temporary. Today's reality does not need to be tomorrow's reality. Tomorrow's reality can be today's dream. The realest thing about you is your dream. What vision do you have for your future? Set up your future today with your dream.

Dreams involve emotions. What makes you angry? What ticks you off? You see, anger is a good thing if you channel it in the right direction. For example, I'm angry about drugs. I hate drugs. I want to put every drug dealer in prison, lock them up and throw away the key. That's why I ran a drug rehab centre for five years. I was passionate about it, and I still am and will be until the day I die. You've got to be emotionally involved with your vision, but being emotional is not enough. You must take action, one step at a time in the right direction, and stick to it. Get moved and then get moving!

Your dream and your passions are linked. Passion means eagerness, excitement, fervor, fire, intensity, rapture, joy, spirit, zest and zeal! Put all that into your life, your career, your business and your relationships. Put that into creating your wealth.

What moves you?

What is it that stirs and drives you? Let me warn you that if you're not moved by your dream, nobody else will be. If you're not passionate about prosperity, you're never going to prosper. Passion isn't about being loud. Passion is a way of doing things. You won't make money, you won't make progress in any area, without passion. Why? Because passion leads to productivity, productivity leads to profit, profit leads to pleasure, and pleasure brings you back to passion. If you lose any of the elements in this sequence, you will lose your passion. My friend Gary Zelesky puts it this way: 'Your passion in life creates your position in life.'

So what's your passion? Your passion and your dream go together. While prosperity is the consequence, passion is the cause.

Despite what some philosophers will try to tell you, you are not an amoeba in the cosmos floating aimlessly around the universe. You and I are much, much more than that. You were designed for a purpose. Your goal is to find that purpose. When you find it, you'll find all the rest: the passion, eagerness, excitement, fervor, fire, intensity, rapture, joy, spirit, zest and zeal!

You and I have only one life. So let me ask you: what is going to define your life? In 10 or 20 years from now, what will your life look like? Will you be defined by abundance or poverty, increase or lack, generosity or scarcity?

The Creator wired us with a desire to succeed. I believe that's what Bruce Springsteen meant when he sang about everyone having 'a hungry heart'. We all hunger to be loved, to love others, to be cared for and to care for others. And connected to that is a hunger to succeed. That's why we see ourselves in movie heroes. I don't know about you, but over the years I've been Rocky Balboa, Conan the Barbarian, Captain Kirk...and Bambi (just kidding!). The hero inside us always comes out.

The birth of my dream

I had a dream when I was 15 years old. I'd walked into a Christian youth gathering and it was so boring that even boring people called it boring. They were singing songs like 'Kumbaya' and 'Give Me Oil in My Lamp'. I looked around the audience and saw three cats, two dogs and a flea...and a few teenagers. As I sat there, the preacher began shouting, 'Flee fornication!' I didn't know what that was, so I turned to my mate Sam and said, 'I don't know what a fornication is, man, but when I find one I'm going to run! This guy's scaring the hell out of me!'

Sam looked at me and replied, 'Pat, he's talking about sex before marriage.'

'Well why didn't he say that? Why say "fleeeeee foooooooornication"?'

I remember sitting there thinking, *This is supposed to influence young people?* I looked around and saw how irrelevant everything was—the music, the songs, the message and the environment. Sitting there that night I had a dream...of auditoriums that were full of young people standing singing songs that actually meant something to them. I heard a voice in my heart saying to me, 'You are going to take over this youth event one day.' My immediate response was, 'Good! Someone needs to!' and then, 'And I'm going to fire every musician and everyone in the choir!' The weird part was that I wasn't even a Christian at the time. I was a young gangster who had been invited to this youth rally for the first time. But I caught a vision of what it could be.

Twelve years later, when I was 27 years old, 350 young people turned up at my first meeting. We played rock music and had smoke machines and coloured lights on the stage. We had band members who had performed with groups like Air Supply and Rose Tattoo. One of my speakers was a guy called Big Chick who had once worked as a bodyguard for Prince. Many parents called it the devil's music. They told me God's music was country and western. One day a minister came to me and declared, 'A snowflake in hell has more chance of survival than a kid listening to you and your drivel.' Six months later, after his son had come to my meeting and given up heroin, the minister came up to me and said, 'I think some snowflakes can come out of hell and survive.' The minister changed his tune when his son was helped.

People will want to criticise your dream

There will always be people who want to criticise your dream or steal it away from you. You'll meet no opposition until you get a dream — then all the knives come out! Watch out for these people. There is a touching scene in the movie *The Pursuit of Happyness* in which Chris (played by Will Smith) tells his son (Smith's real son, by the way): 'Hey, don't ever let somebody tell you that you can't do something. Not even me, alright? Alright! You got a dream? You gotta protect it. People can't do something themselves, they want to tell you that you can't do it. You want something? Then go get it, period!' There are many out there who will tell you why you *can't* do something rather than why you *can*. You are the only one who can give them permission to steal your dream from you. It's up to you.

Then there are others who will want to sell you *their* dreams. There was a man whose father wanted him to be a carpenter while his mother wanted him to be a policeman. They enrolled him in carpentry school and he was a failure. So he tried police training, but that didn't work out either. But then he walked into a gymnasium and his eyes lit up: he saw herculean men pumping weights and knew this was it. He wanted to be a body builder. One day, walking past a newspaper stand, he noticed a photo of the first actor to play the lead role in a Hercules movie. His name was Reg Park. In that moment he said to himself, *If Reg Park can do it, so can I!* Reg Park would become his mentor.

At 18, he won the Mr Europe bodybuilding contest. He won the title again the following year. The next he became Mr Universe. He won the Mr Olympia title seven times. He decided he wanted to become a movie star and went on to play the lead in movies such as *Conan the Barbarian, The Terminator, Predator* and *Total Recall*. His name, of course, is Arnold Schwarzenegger. Like Arnie, you can't live everyone else's dream. You have to find your own.

It's amazing how parents try to live their own dreams through their children. Like many Italian parents, my dad wanted me to learn to play the piano accordion. I mean, come on! How many piano accordion players do you know who attract the girls? They know how to push buttons all right, but not the *right* buttons! I just did not want to end up being the wedding singer at Italian weddings.

Don't compare your dream to others'

If you want to fulfil your dream, don't compare yourself to others'. It's like a cow staring at a milk truck with signs plastered all over it saying *homogenised, pasteurised, standardised, with vitamin A*... The cow looks at that truck and says, 'That's making me feel a little bit inadequate right now.' You are uniquely gifted. Don't compare your dream to other people's dreams. It is so easy to celebrate another's uniqueness and devalue your own. Begin to value what you have.

Now, back to *my* dream...Within a few years I helped build Youth Alive into the largest youth organisation in Australia. We packed out some of Australia's biggest stadiums in Sydney, Melbourne, Brisbane and Perth. I became a motivational speaker, addressing crowds of up to 70 000 people at a time. At the age of 35, I stood in front of the Washington Monument and addressed a crowd of a quarter of a million people and a television audience estimated at 14 million. I ran one of Australia's most successful drug and alcohol rehabilitation centres. I had a weekly national television program. I was one of the lead pastors of the largest church in Australia, Hillsong Church. Today I have sold more than 700 000 copies of my books and well over two million copies of my CDs. That's my story. My dream came true, and so can yours! You're the main character in the story or dream of your life. You can change the plot midway through. You can decide on a different ending, just like one of those movies that offers two endings, but you must be the director.

> You're the main character in the story or dream of your life.

There's a biblical story of a young man called Joseph who had a dream that his father and his brothers would one day bow before him. His brothers grew jealous of his dream and sold him as a slave. A group called the Midianites then sold him to an Egyptian guy called Potiphar. When this 17 year old appeared before Potiphar he was naked, bruised, starving and in chains, yet he is described as a prosperous man, because in his dream Joseph saw himself as much more than a slave, and sure enough he became what he saw in himself—a very wealthy, influential man. Deep down, how do you see yourself? Be honest. Do you see your dream becoming reality? Do you own your dream?

There's a phenomenon called the Pygmalion effect that acts rather like a self-fulfilling prophecy. If you've seen the movie *My Fair Lady*, then you've seen this principle in action. A man takes an impoverished London street girl and trains her to look and sound like a princess. His goal is to present her at a society ball and to convince the guests that she was born and raised as a lady. After exhausting training, Eliza slowly learns how to talk and act like a lady. Then the Pygmalion effect kicks in. Eliza begins to see herself differently, as does her teacher. Her transformation is complete. The ball finally arrives and Eliza is accepted into society in triumph.

What image of your wealth dominates your life?

Your net worth seldom exceeds your self-worth. The truth is that how you see yourself will determine how others see you. If you see yourself as getting by with just enough to live on, to make ends meet, then that's how others will see you too. What image of you, your wealth, your business and your career dominates your life?

One of the reasons I created annual events such as La Dolce Vita at the Palazzo Versace Luxury Hotel on Australia's Gold Coast and Wealth Warrior (see p. 159 for details) was to help people to see themselves in a different light, to see themselves at another level. It's not about class or social hierarchy; it's about seeing yourself differently.

The other reason why these events are so powerful is that sometimes you have got to taste your dream first. When you come to these events you will taste, feel, smell, touch and hear a life of wealth. I want you to have a go. I love giving people little insights into what their life could be, because then it becomes easier for them to believe they can get there. The route to my office takes me past a cemetery, and sometimes as I pass I think to myself, *We all end up there!* But then I think, *While I'm here I might as well live my life!* Don't die with your dream still inside you, unlived. Don't die with words like 'I should have' or 'I would have' on your lips.

A friend of mine used to collect fine wines. He would show me and his family these beautiful bottles and say, 'I'm waiting for a special day to open up these.' One day his son was killed in a tragic car accident, aged just 23. It completely changed his perspective on life. He later told me, 'I remember my son used to ask me, "Hey Dad, can we open up one of those bottles?" And I'd respond, "No son, I'm waiting for a special occasion." His 18th birthday came and went. I never opened a bottle. His 21st birthday came and went, and I didn't open a bottle. I was waiting for a special day.'

'How do you feel about that now?' I asked him.

He replied, 'I've come to realise that every day is a special day. I won't put off until tomorrow what I can do today.'

Live your life now. Every day is a special day. Get a dream — one that's your very own — and start heading down the road to that dream. Decide to prosper! To do so, you have to focus on what you want. You have to make a decision, a commitment. Nothing happens in life until you make a decision. Decide today:

I am committed to becoming prosperous!

I am committed to building wealth!

I am committed to building a great business!

I am committed to building a beautiful home!

I am committed to saving for my retirement!

No matter who you are, what you know or don't know about money and wealth, what your current circumstances are, and what has happened to you in the past, if you make a firm decision today to do something to change your world, then you are at the starting line of your journey towards a prosperous life.

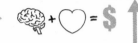

Take steps now towards your destination

If you're having trouble seeing your future, or if you're not sure what your dream is or should be, here are two exercises to help you.

1   Write down three things you are passionate about. Then beside each one write your vision for it—in other words, what can you see yourself doing in each of these three areas?

a _____

b _____

c _____

2   Close your eyes and paint a picture in your mind of what you want your life to look like 10 years from now. Don't be restricted by your present circumstances. Give yourself permission to dream. What's your family like? What are your kids like? What does your business or career look like? What kind of home are you living in? What is your financial world like? What community involvement do you have? What do your hobbies and holidays look like? In summary, how do you live?

Chapter 3

What's it gonna take?
A reality check

One day, after speaking at an event, I was approached by a woman who was clearly distraught. One of my tenets is that you 'make as much as you can, save as much as you can and give as much as you can'. She challenged this advice, arguing that it's impossible to do all three. I told her that for 200 people in the room this news came too late, as they were already doing it. The reason she couldn't see it was she was a third-generation welfare recipient and was used to getting as much as she could without working or saving. As we argued on stage she became increasingly frustrated and, at the same time, honest. When I suggested her financial problems might owe something to her welfare mentality she screamed at the top of her voice. I loved her response. She wiped away the tears and said, 'F*** being broke! I don't want to be broke any more!' At that point someone in the audience came up to me and offered to pay for her financial education and get her started with a new business idea.

When we met up a year later she told me she had made $150 000 profit through her business. What a turnaround! Sometimes you just have to face the truth and declare, 'Enough's enough! I don't want to do this any more!' When you say it like that you draw a line in the sand that says, 'That's it! I'm not going down that path any longer! I'm changing direction!'

Most of us just get used to a certain way of life. We get stuck there. We want more, we're hungry for more, but we never do anything to get ourselves out of our comfort zone. Bono and U2 put it eloquently in their song 'Stuck in a Moment'. Every one of us gets stuck in a moment. We get stuck in moments of our childhood when people told us we will never amount to much. We get stuck in moments of 'I can't afford it!' or 'I wish I could!' or 'I could never do that!' We get stuck there and we get comfortable with its familiarity.

The truth will set you free

Right now your comfort zone may feel like a prison cell that's holding you back, a cell made up of *can'ts* and *mustn'ts*. You're surrounded by unfounded fears and phobias. Every fear you have — the fear of failure, the fear of breaking down, the fear of not being able to make do — is like a bar in your prison cell. You have to break out of that prison.

Living fearlessly is not the same thing as never being afraid.

Living fearlessly is not the same thing as never being afraid. It's good to be afraid occasionally. Fear is a great teacher. What is *not* good is living in fear, allowing fear to dictate your choices, allowing fear to define who you are. Living fearlessly means standing up to fear, taking its measure, refusing to let it shape and define your life. Living fearlessly means taking risks, taking gambles, not playing it safe. It means refusing to take no for an answer and saying yes to your dreams. Take a risk, take a gamble, pay the price for your dream.

Are you sick of being stuck at your current level of prosperity? Are you frustrated by the lack in your life, by your small-thinking, poverty-bound mindset? We all tend to navigate by what we tolerate. When we tolerate things in our life that hold us back, we find ourselves constantly making excuses for being the way we are. But if we stop tolerating this mindset, then we'll stop navigating that way and instead we'll begin to instigate new habits, new behaviours and new ways of thinking. We will never change what we consistently tolerate.

Some people are always complaining about their lives. They say things like:

'I'm sick of never having enough money!'

'I hate not being able to afford music lessons for my kids!'

'I'm tired of my old car!'

'I don't like my bad spending habits!'

How often do you catch yourself saying things like this? As much as you might deplore certain things in your life, the truth is you don't really hate them enough, because if you really hated them you wouldn't tolerate them. Your prosperity is handicapped by what you won't give up.

'I'm not staying here any longer!'

The first step towards becoming more prosperous is to make the decision and declare, 'I am not staying here any longer!' If your desire for something greater doesn't drive you to change, then a crisis generally will. Don't wait for the crisis. Take control of your destiny now.

For years Beth and Andrew had been living beyond their means. No-one around them knew it. Perhaps they didn't realise it themselves. Andrew worked in the building trade. Before they had children, Beth had been an assistant manager in a major department store. When the kids came along, Beth chose to give up her job to focus on raising their two children. But moving from two incomes to one didn't change their lifestyle much. They continued to eat out with friends at expensive restaurants. Each year the family took an overseas holiday. The children always had the latest electronic toys and gadgets. They had a large mortgage on their beautiful new two-storey house in an exclusive suburb. Over the years, as the property market boomed, they refinanced their home a number of times to help pay for their lifestyle, each time increasing the size of their debt.

By the time Andrew came to see me, he had put his house on the market. He knew they would have to sell it at a loss — in other words, their house was now worth less than their mortgage. And they faced the prospect of not being able to own their own home for many years to come. As he reeled off his financial problems, I couldn't help thinking, *Andrew, you didn't see this coming?* The truth was they had been spending more than they were earning for a long time. Notice that that's a path? They weren't just making independent financial decisions over the years — they were taking steps in a certain direction. They were on a pathway towards financial disaster. They just didn't see it that way at the time.

Beth and Andrew are not alone — not by a long shot! Sadly, I know many others in their situation. You might respond, 'But they should have seen the warning signs and cut back on their expenses!' Well, you're right. So how about you? What path are you on? What financial steps have you been taking? It's time for a reality check. Take a look in the mirror. If you don't do it now, you might regret it later. It's time to face the fact: *you* are responsible for your current situation just as much as Andrew and Beth were responsible for theirs.

So what's it going to take to reach your financial goals? To begin with, it will take a determined effort to avoid taking pathways leading *away* from your financial dream. Other routes can be so very appealing. We are constantly bombarded by clever advertisements enticing us to make bad financial decisions:

Don't pay a thing till Christmas!

Now more affordable than ever!

You've worked hard — you deserve it!

Free upgrades!

Buy one, get one free!

You're worth it!

I'm not saying that if you accept one of these deals you'll go bankrupt, but if you continue to allow yourself to be suckered into such schemes you will most likely arrive at a destination you never intended to visit. I don't want you to go there and I don't think you do either.

Truth quest vs happiness quest

So what's it going to take? The next time you face a financial decision, make a decision to follow a truth quest rather than a happiness quest. Our problem stems from the fact that most of us are not on a truth quest — that is, we don't wake up every morning with a burning desire to know what's true, what's right and what's honourable. Instead, we are on a happiness quest. We want to be happy, and our quest for happiness often defeats our pursuit of what's true.

If you have perfectly good clothes you never wear hanging in your closet, but you plan to do a little clothes shopping later this week, then you are on a happiness quest. Why would you buy more clothes when you don't wear the ones you have? Because when you wear something new and stylish you feel better about yourself. In other words, you're happy. When you put on last year's clothes, you feel a bit last-yearish, unhappy, and you don't want to feel that way. So the next time you head for the mall, admit that you aren't simply shopping for clothes — you're on a happiness quest. The same goes for cars, houses, computers, smartphones, TV sets . . . We want the latest and greatest because they make us feel happy, comfortable and contented. Truth, on the other hand, can be uncomfortable and painful. Sometimes truth is so painful we would rather run away than embrace it.

'The truth shall make you free,' the Bible tells us. Following a truth quest will eventually free you from the burden of worry and anxiety. Following a happiness quest will simply delay the inevitable. Your current financial problems won't go away by ignoring them. In fact, they will get worse! You've got to face them and fix them. You've got to take responsibility for your life.

Dreams generally don't start with reality; they start with desire and possibility. But we do need a reality check sometimes, especially those of us who say, 'I might just get lucky!' or 'I'm waiting for my lucky break.' Look, if you're depending on luck to fulfil your dreams, then, well, good luck to you, because very few people achieve their dreams that way. According to the operators of the UK National Lottery, only 55 per cent of winners are happier after winning. Almost 40 per cent of the families of the winners admit to being less happy after their windfall. Sadly, almost 45 per cent of lottery winners spend their entire winnings within five years. In other words, a lotto win is not all it is cracked up to be.

Are you a cause person or an effect person?

Shallow people believe in luck; strong people believe in cause and effect. In life, you are going to be either an effect person (forever affected by and reacting to the things around you) or a cause person (who causes things to happen). Here's the difference:

When a crisis hits, an effect person feels like a victim, but a cause person responds with a decision.

When something goes wrong, an effect person blames others, but a cause person takes full responsibility.

An effect person lives by consequence; a cause person creates results.

An effect person will go only so far and then give up; a cause person does whatever it takes.

An effect person suffers analysis paralysis; a cause person takes action.

There's a crucial difference between fantasisers and dream builders too:

A fantasiser relies on luck; a dream builder relies on discipline.

A fantasiser focuses on the destination; a dream builder focuses on the direction of the pathway.

A fantasiser cultivates unhealthy expectations; a dream builder cultivates healthy discontent.

A fantasiser minimises the value of work; a dream builder values action.

A fantasiser waits for things to happen; a dream builder initiates action.

Where are you now?

When you are lost you don't need to be motivated to go faster; you need to stop, identify where you are and change direction accordingly. So where do you stand right now? Geographically speaking, you can't get to where you want to go unless you know where you are now. In the same way, you can't get to where you want to be financially until you are willing to admit where you are to begin with. On your path to prosperity from A to Z, where are you right now? Be brutally honest with yourself. When you deceive yourself, you blind yourself to your current location. People who are geographically lost claim:

'Everything is fine.'

'We'll get there soon.'

'I can handle this.'

'It's all going to be all right.'

I was saying those words when I lost my way en route to the Los Angeles International Airport a few years ago. For most of that trip I was in self-denial. That kind of self-talk doesn't help when you are lost on a highway, and it's even less helpful when you are lost financially. All it does is encourage you to keep moving in the wrong direction and get even more lost.

The starting point of your dream is wherever you are right now.

To find the financial path that will take you where you want to go, you have to break the cycle of self-deception. If you continue to hide behind excuses, you will never have the vision or strength to do a 180-degree turn and move in a whole new direction. The starting point of your dream is wherever you are right now. You'll never get to where you want to go without being clear about where that is, but it's only when you know where you are now that you can work out the direction you need to take.

There's a cost to your dream

To achieve your financial goals, first you need to understand that pursuing your dreams is going to cost you. Dreams themselves are free, but their fulfilment requires sacrifice. Look at anyone who ever saw their dream fulfilled and you'll see that it always cost them something. Martin Luther King Jr had a dream, but it cost him his life.

Amy Tan had a dream to become an author, but this American daughter of Chinese immigrants was told she didn't have what it took to become a writer. She asked her boss if she could take on more writing tasks so she could learn to write better. He said no. When she persisted, he fired her, declaring, 'You'll never make a dime writing!' Amy Tan set out to prove him wrong. Working from home, she took on as many freelance writing assignments as she could, sometimes working 90 hours a week. Eventually she wrote a novel called *The Joy Luck Club*. She went on to publish several other best-selling novels, including *The Kitchen God's Wife* and *The Hundred Secret Senses*. Today Amy Tan is one of America's best-loved authors. There was a cost to her dream, but she decided it was worth it.

It may cost you some friendships, it may cost you a change of thinking, it may cost you a whole lot of things, but any dream worth pursuing is worth paying a price for. It's amazing how many people allow their dreams to be shattered by a few challenges or obstacles. We have all faced challenges. I know I have! The fulfilment of dreams involves heartache and struggle. That's part of what makes achieving your dream so worthwhile.

A few years ago I had a dream of raising hundreds of thousands of dollars for the drug rehabilitation centre I oversaw in Sydney, through a sponsored run. I decided to run from Sydney to Woollongong, a distance of about 80 kilometres (50 miles), in two days. We called it 'Running for their lives'. A few boys from the rehab centre joined me along the route. During the run I damaged the ITB muscle in my leg, making it extremely hard to run. I had to have shots in my leg to cope with the pain, but I figured I didn't have to break any records, I just had to finish the course. I determined that if I couldn't run it I could walk it, and if I couldn't walk I was going to crawl. I finished the run, damaged leg and all. With hundreds of sponsors, we raised $180 000 for the centre. I decided I was never going to run that distance again.

The following year I ran from Coffs Harbour to Sydney in six straight days, a distance of about 530 kilometres (330 miles). We raised $186 000 that year. In total the 610 kilometres (380 miles) I ran helped raise almost $370 000 for the rehab centre.

What was the cost of my dream? For a start, while my body would be perfect as a garden gnome, it isn't built for running. So I had to train extra hard to be able to withstand the gruelling pounding on bitumen roads. Today my legs are paying the price of those two runs. I take magnesium tablets and stretch my legs two to three times a day to avoid further deterioration to my leg muscles. I also suffer constant lower back pain. That is the cost I have had to pay. It is a big cost, but the reward is even bigger. That $370 000 helped more than 400 young men free themselves from drugs. Many of the boys who took part in those runs with me are now young businessmen and entrepreneurs inspiring others. Others are church and community leaders. Today some of them are self-made millionaires. Was my dream worth the cost? Without a doubt!

Are you willing to pay the price?

The question is, are you willing to pay the price of your dream? At some point, we have to transition from believing in the dream to actually buying into the dream. That takes a whole new level of commitment, because suddenly you need to invest in that dream.

When I wrote my first book, *Wake Up and Dream*, I had no idea it would sell so many copies. I remember back then making a commitment that I would give away the proceeds of the first order that came in — every cent — to Youth Alive, the youth organisation I was director of at the time. I thought my first order would be about 500 books, so mentally I was prepared to donate that amount of money. But the first order that came in was for 27 000 copies! I had to take a step back and accept the fact that if I was to stick to my commitment I would now be donating a *lot* of money!

At that time I didn't own a home. In fact, I had my eye on some land in a suburb in north-western Sydney. I wanted to build the family home on that block of land, but I didn't have enough money for the deposit. So when the cheque arrived, my wife opened the envelope and pulled it out. The amount was $197 000! Suddenly we faced a dilemma. She looked at the amount and then looked at me and said, 'Well, what about the land?'

'The land has to wait,' I replied. 'The dream comes first.' I signed over that $197 000 to the drug rehab centre. Let me tell you, that was the hardest signature I have ever had to write. Now here's the miracle: I ended up building my house and land for $480 000 — a price that was unheard of at that time. I got my dream home for a bargain, but it cost me something first.

So what's it going to take to reach your financial goals? We have a choice either to play now and pay later, or to pay now and play later. The younger you are when you invest, the more you will have when you reach retirement age. Unfortunately, most of us aren't willing to pay the price when we are young, but if we don't start paying the price early, our dream is going to cost us more later. The price needs to be paid sooner rather than later.

> The price needs to be paid sooner rather than later.

Turn your pain into gain

Contrary to some popular ideologies, the universe won't bring your dream to you. You've got to take action. You've got to go and get it yourself. Your creator gave you a brain, so use it. You may have faced some challenges in your life that set you back and limited your wealth potential, but I'll let loose and tell it to you straight: stop sucking lemons. Stop sucking your thumb. Don't play blamititis or victim any longer. I have yet to meet a rich victim. Get up and take responsibility for your wealth, because whatever pain you have today you can turn into a profit tomorrow. You can turn your pain into gain.

Australian actor and comedian Paul Hogan once quipped, 'I bit off more than I could chew, so I chewed as fast as I could.' Have you ever bitten off more than you can chew? Here's my advice: keep on chewing. When you put yourself into a position in which you have no choice but to make something work, you do all you can to make it work. The lesson here is this: the price of your dream is generally higher than you initially planned.

Muhammad Ali found he had bitten off more than he could chew when he agreed to fight Sonny Liston for the heavyweight title in 1964. Everyone agreed Liston was going to beat Ali up in the ring. Liston was a tough ex-con with apparent mob connections. When the man punched a wall, he put a hole through it. Ali was absolutely frightened of him, so how did he respond? During the pre-fight buildup Ali went on the offensive with words. He and his entourage would visit Liston's training session every day to tease him. Ali called him a 'big, ugly bear'. Liston thought Ali was a nutcase. Right up until fight night there was an incredible tension between the two boxers. Against the odds Muhammad Ali won that fight. How did he beat Liston? It wasn't his strength. What outsmarted Liston was that Ali went on the attack. He had painted himself into a corner when he took on that fight, but he absorbed that pressure and turned it into something positive.

What's it going to take to reach your financial goals? You've got to put in a little extra effort. Those who succeed generally don't pay a lot more than everyone else — they just pay a *little* more than everyone else. Sometimes it's just that little extra effort that makes all the difference. It's that little bit of extra studying, making those small extra repayments, that little bit of extra saving that nobody else wants to do.

Cultivate the right habits

Remember, life is nothing more than the sum total of many successful years. A successful year is nothing more than the sum total of 12 successful months. A successful month is nothing more than the sum total of four successful weeks. A successful week is nothing more than the sum total of seven successful days. Practising the right financial habits day in and day out turns into successful habits every week, then every month, then every year. Successful financial habits over the years will undoubtedly keep you on the right path towards a prosperous future. Good habits will cause you to win over and over again. Cultivate the right habits and practise them daily. What you do daily will determine what you become permanently. Commit every day to listen to an audio message on prosperity. Commit every day to read a chapter or an article about prosperity. Commit every day to read about the lives of prosperous people.

A young German musician wanted to be a conductor but his style was odd to say the least. When conducting soft passages he would drop into a crouch. When the music called for a crescendo, he'd leap into the air with a shout. On one occasion he jumped to cue a dramatic passage, but the musicians didn't respond. He had lost track of his place and had jumped too soon. The musicians began looking to the first violinist for direction instead of to the erratic young conductor. His memory wasn't very good either. During one performance he tried to conduct the orchestra through a section of the music he had earlier instructed them to skip. When they didn't play the passage he stopped conducting altogether and shouted, 'Stop! Wrong! That will not do! Again! Again! Again!'

Everything about him was clumsy. When he conducted a piano concerto, he knocked some candles off the piano he was playing. During another concert he knocked over a choir boy and left him unconscious on the floor. The musicians begged him to give up his dream of becoming a great conductor. Finally he listened — and Ludwig van Beethoven went on to become one of the greatest composers of all time. Someone had to tell him, 'Stop! This is your strength here! Concentrate on what you are good at!'

To achieve your financial dream you have to build on your strengths. Don't waste time and energy on the things you are not good at. You'll only get frustrated and annoy everyone around you. Building on your strengths will give you consistently good results and the highest return for your efforts.

12 steps to get you back on track

You are wherever you are in life right now as a result of the sum total of the choices you have made up to this point. So if you are not satisfied with where you are, it's imperative that you change direction to get a better quality of life. It's your responsibility to choose wisely so you don't repeat the same errors again.

At the drug rehabilitation centre in Sydney our slogan was 'Turning nightmares into dreams'. These men had not set out to become addicts and destroy their lives. They had mothers, fathers, brothers and sisters who watched them make wrong choices. Some of them even had wives and children who ended up sharing the pain of addiction. Despite their best intentions, these young men made decisions that took them in a direction they never wanted to go, but the steps they took were their own responsibility, no-one else's.

Like you, they came to a point where they decided to face reality. They were prepared for the truth, and the truth pointed them in another direction. They realised that to head in that new direction they needed to make some very difficult decisions. Like Muhammad Ali, they decided they had to fight their way out of a tight corner. The steps they took from that moment began to lead them in the direction of their dreams. To this day I am so proud of those men. Their lives had spiralled out of control until they felt they had no hope of ever realising their faded dreams, but they decided to fight back by taking daily steps in the right direction.

One of the keys to their success was what we called the 12-step program. This step-by-step process is not a solution, it's a path, a series of commitments, that will take you in the right direction. It worked for these young men, and I know it will work for you too, if you follow each step every day.

First, let me give you 12 steps *not* to take—12 patterns of thought that are sure to lead to financial disaster.

12 steps to financial disaster

- You don't think you can improve financially and/or you don't think there is anything wrong with your financial situation.

- You believe your financial situation will work itself out without you having to change much.

- You believe your financial situation is mostly out of your control.

- You think you are smarter than you really are.

- You won't listen to wise financial advice, especially if it takes you out of your comfort zone.

- You want a quick-fix solution, not a step-by-step process.

- You believe you don't need anyone else's help.

- You believe your situation is not your fault and that you are the victim of other people's actions.

- You don't believe that your financial situation has been influenced by those with whom you associate on a regular basis.

- You fail to recognise and address issues you have with money.

- You don't believe in financial principles, such as sowing what you reap and generosity.

- You aren't willing to change your current habits, patterns and behaviours regarding money.

Now, if instead you make the following commitments, I believe you will experience a financial awakening:

12 steps to financial prosperity

- I recognise I have problems with money and my finances have become unmanageable.

- I am prepared to do all I can to improve my financial position.

- I am prepared to ask for advice to help me restore my financial situation.

- I am committed to turning my financial situation over to someone who knows better.

- I am committed to making a fearless inventory of the bad decisions I have made up to this point in order to learn from my mistakes.

- I admit that I have taken steps down the wrong pathway/s.

- I am committed to learning all I can about better money management.

- I will assess my friendships and commit to spending more time with people who have healthy financial habits.

- I am ready and willing to cast off wrong mindsets about money.

- I am ready and willing to renounce wrong behaviours regarding money.

- I am committed to making a list of all the people I may have harmed financially in the past and to make amends to them all.

- I am committed to building wealth over the long term.

Take steps now to get back on track

Be honest with yourself about where you are now financially. Write down a list that summarises your current financial status—for example, your school loans, credit card debt, excessive car lease and uncontrolled budget.

My starting location:

_____

_____

_____

_____

Now write down where you want to end up financially. Take your time, and get excited about it. For example: 'I want to end up debt free, with no mortgage on my home, with enough money for our retirement and to support my favourite charity...'

My final location:

_____

_____

_____

Then consider your potential to reach your dream. How far away are you from where you want to be? Compare your debts with your assets, and consider your time frame too. How many years do you have left to reach your financial goals?

Also take stock of your weaknesses—the things that have been preventing you from moving forward financially. Perhaps you hate budgets and tend to spend more than you earn. Maybe you overindulge in what others would call excesses, such as the latest electronic gadgets, a brand-new car or a king-size barbecue...in fact, a king-size anything!

Remember, between yesterday's regret and tomorrow's dream is today's opportunity. Make the most of it!

Chapter 4

Will you choose to change your world?
It's decision time

When he was a boy, former US president Ronald Reagan was taken to a cobbler for a new pair of shoes. The cobbler looked at the boy and asked, 'Do you want square toes or round toes?' Unable to decide, the boy didn't answer, so the cobbler told him to come back in a few days with a decision. Several days later the cobbler saw him on the street and asked him again what style of toes he wanted on his shoes. Young Ronald still couldn't decide, so the shoemaker replied, 'Well, come by in a couple of days. Your shoes will be ready.' When the boy entered the cobbler's shop, he found one square-toed shoe and one round-toed shoe! The cobbler said, 'This will teach you never to let other people make decisions for you.'

You need to make a firm decision today. You must decide to do something to change your financial world. Once you have made that critical decision, you will be at the starting line of your journey towards prosperity. The exciting truth in this is that the starting point to your journey towards prosperity is wherever you are right now. It doesn't matter who you are, what your current circumstances are, or what has happened to you in the past. It doesn't even matter what you know or don't know about money and wealth. Once you have made that decision, you can begin to move towards a prosperous future.

Genuine prosperity does not generally happen by accident. It takes a decision on your part to become prosperous and then it takes a pattern of right decisions to find wealth. You have to decide to make a commitment to prosperity. If you're not fully committed to becoming prosperous, you can't blame anyone or anything else for your failure. Your upbringing, your job, your organisation and your education are not responsible. If you want to prosper, there's only one person who matters — *you*! You have to decide that you are going to be a person of wealth.

Author and management consultant Peter Drucker writes: 'Wherever you see a successful business, someone once made a courageous decision.' The Laboratory of Psychological Studies of the Stevens Institute of Technology, New Jersey, once conducted a study of unsuccessful executives in more than 200 firms. It found that an inability to make decisions is one of the principal reasons executives fail and a much more common reason for failure than a lack of specific knowledge or technical know-how.

If you want to prosper, you have to decide what you want. You have to choose. If you don't know what you want, how will you recognise it when you see it? This decision is critical to starting down the road to a prosperous future. The principle of the path tells us that the decisions you make right now will affect you somewhere down the track — it's a snowball effect. The decisions on spending or saving you made in your younger years will affect you financially in later years. Your financial decisions have a huge impact on your future.

Emotional decisions are hard to resist

In *The Principle of the Path*, Andy Stanley writes: 'I learned a long time ago that there is something more important than being right, and that is making the right decision.' Sometimes that means avoiding an emotional decision. *Should I sign that two-year telephone-and-internet deal and receive a free smartphone?* If you're crazy about smartphones, then it's going to be very hard for you to resist making an emotional decision in this situation, overcommitting to high monthly payments just to get a free mobile. Or perhaps you're asking yourself, *Should I take my family on that skiing holiday we've always wanted, even though we can't afford it right now? After all, we've worked so hard this year — we deserve a reward.* Emotional decisions are so hard to resist, aren't they!

But, later on in the book Andy says, 'Ask yourself, What outcome am I expecting from this decision? Does the option I'm considering naturally lead to that outcome?' He goes on to say, 'When you push past the emotion and ask, What outcome do I desire? and Will this option get me there? the answers become painfully clear.'

There are times when you will have to decide to take extreme action — maybe cut up some credit cards, cut back on your entertainment costs, cancel your cable TV service, change jobs, even sell the house — to get yourself back on the right financial path. Yet imagine what kind of a financial pathway you would find yourself on if you did all of the above! There are people around you who would give an arm and a leg to be able to retrace their steps and take some or all of those actions in order to extract themselves from their current circumstances, but many can't do that. They dream of going back in time and making the tough decisions, but they can't. If you're not yet in their shoes, count your blessings. This week, make a decision to put your financial house in order.

Choose the best realistic destination you can aim for

Andy Stanley offers us a reality check in *The Principle of the Path* when he says:

> We can retrace our steps, but we can't turn back the hands of the clock. We can make better choices next time, but we can't go back and do anything about the first time. Time, bad decisions, and experience put some destinations out of reach. There are dreams that can't come true. There are fortunes that are lost for good.

He goes on to say:

> What do you do with the dreams that can't come true?...What do you do when it dawns on you that there are destinations you will never reach?...Some are unreachable because of a single decision. Some destinations are out of reach because of mistakes we've made. Some are out of reach because of decisions others made... I believe everybody faces this kind of disappointment at some point. So what are we supposed to do? Decide to change. Get real. Face facts. Choose the best realistic destination you can now aim for.

I'm sure there are some decisions you would love to go back and change, but you know you can't. That's life. The good news is that we *can* recalibrate our destination and begin moving again. We *can* readjust our financial goals and find the right path to lead us there. The decision you have to make today is this: *I will avoid making the same decisions that led me down the wrong path and start down the right path towards a better financial future.* If you make that one decision, you are halfway there.

There are some things in life that we have no power over, but don't let that stall your forward momentum towards a prosperous future. For example, your business partner may have abused your trust and taken money that was rightfully yours. You didn't choose for that to happen, yet it may have destroyed you financially. But you can still choose how to respond and move on, as difficult as that may be. The power you have now is the power to respond. You have a decision to make.

'Have I made the right decision?'

Many people worry about whether they have made the right decision. They spend much anxious time and energy pondering the decision they've just made. *How do I know I've made the right decision?* To begin with, after you have made a decision, rather than worrying about it, start to make it work for you. You can make a decision better or worse. For example, joining a gym is a good decision, but what makes it better is to show up there regularly! Starting a relationship is also generally a good decision, because people aren't meant to be alone, but you then have to work at that relationship. If you don't, you'll compromise your decision. If you sit there worrying about whether you made the right decision and as a result you make no effort to invest in the relationship, then you've wasted the potential of the decision to the detriment of that relationship.

Similarly, making commitments to work on your personal development and to be successful in business or your career are good decisions. It's what you do *after* your decisions that makes them effective or not. What happens if you've made a bad decision? Well, then you have to make another decision to turn it around, and once you've made *that* decision, stop worrying and start working at it.

Confusion kills decisions

Confusion prevents you from progressing towards prosperity. When people get stuck in confusion over a decision, they're in three minds: do they move forward or backward, or do they stay where they are? But you can't move anywhere while you're in neutral. So get out of neutral as quickly as you can. You can't steer a parked car.

Remember, it's not what you know before your decision but what you do after you've made it that's critical. You can do all the due diligence in the world and then make a decision based on your acquired knowledge, but just making that decision doesn't mean it all turns out great. It's what you do afterwards — using wisdom, common sense and action — that really counts.

Of course, there's always the chance of a glitch or hiccup, something you didn't see ahead of time. For example, I decided to buy a house. It was a good financial decision at the time, but since then I've had no end of trouble with the previous owner. One day I found myself saying, *I wish I had never bought that house!* I quickly realised that was one of the stupidest things I've ever said in my life. Why? Because the decision was made, and it was the right decision. I knew that it's what I do next that really matters.

The situation became so difficult that it started to affect me emotionally. I was burning up unnecessary energy. I was getting depressed, jumping at shadows. I battled with it for months, then I thought to myself, *You know what? I don't need to expend energy on this. I need to put it in the hands of an expert who can deal with the issue for me so I can get on with my life.* That's the critical decision I made — to put it in the hands of someone else who was better equipped to deal with it. I had to step up to the plate and remove the stress from my life. I had to make that follow-up decision to avoid having my original decision turn bad.

Prioritise your decisions

The challenge for all of us is that often we are faced with the need to make multiple decisions at once. Have you been in that situation? It can be a nightmare. Often we find that one decision hinges on another and it feels like they're all connected like dominoes. So how do we prioritise all these decisions? If you're going to be prosperous, you have to do it right.

Consider the 'three Rs' when prioritising your decisions: *required, return* and *reward.* First, ask yourself, *What is required of me?* If you're not making decisions and your team, your staff, your associates or your family are on hold, don't blame them for a lack of progress or productivity. Look to yourself, then respond with a decision. Next, ask yourself, *What will give me my greatest return?* In other words, compare the payoffs. Ask, *What will produce the best results for me in the time I have, with the resources and the people I have?* List the returns, from most to least important.

Every week I get phone calls from people who want to have a coffee so they can pump me for advice. Any more coffee meetings and I'm going to end up a mobile espresso bar! I don't meet with everyone—I simply can't. I also know that some of these people want to suck out of me what they can, but at the same time they don't want to invest in me. I'm okay with that, because by nature I'm a giver, but I have to prioritise who I meet with or I won't have time left over for other things. Also, I've found there are some people I can't help:

- I can't help the person who doesn't think she has a problem.

- I can't help the person who thinks *I'm* his problem.

- I can't help the person who wants an emotional connection rather than practical direction.

- I can't help people who have no clear picture of what they want.

- I can't help people who want me to invest time, effort, energy and money in their problems if they don't want to do the same.

Some of us waste so much time on people who aren't prepared to invest back into our lives, and then we wonder where our day went! You've got to guard and prioritise your time. Weigh up what gives you the greatest return on your investment (ROI). Work out where your payoff is.

Third, whenever you make a decision, ask yourself, *Is this going to bring a reward? What is going to be the most rewarding decision? What will give me the most personal satisfaction?* It's important not to skip the first two Rs and go straight to the third one. You have to follow the right sequence if you want to make the right decisions to influence your financial future positively.

There are two more related tips to decision making that I find helpful. First, learn to choose and refuse. In other words, every choice you make requires you to refuse something else. When you stand at the altar with your marriage partner and the minister asks: 'Will you love, honour, comfort and cherish her/him from this day forward, *refusing all others*, keeping only to her/him for as long as you both shall live?', imagine if you replied, 'Hmm, I'm just not sure I can refuse the others. Let me think about it.' With an answer like that, I'm not sure you will be headed in the direction of a great marriage. In the same way, if you want to become healthy, you have to choose healthy, nutritious foods and refuse others, and you have to choose to get up early to go for a morning run and refuse to stay in bed any longer.

> A kilogram of diamonds and a kilogram of dirt weigh the same, but one is far more valuable than the other.

Second, choose the things you value. A kilogram of diamonds and a kilogram of dirt weigh the same, but one is far more valuable than the other. What do you value in life? Do you value a great lifestyle and financial freedom? If you do, you need to decide what that means to you. Once you know what you value, it becomes easier to make a decision.

We have to make critical decisions about our financial goals. Ask yourself, *What am I trying to achieve financially? What is essential to my business or my job?* So many times we get stuck in the non-essentials. Sound familiar? We get involved in the tyranny of the urgent, rather than the importance of our goals and growth. We get sidetracked by minor stuff. Don't veer away from your objectives — from what you're trying to achieve financially for yourself and your family. Sometimes the easiest thing to do in life is the very thing you're *not* supposed to be doing, but that will divert you from the path you should be on.

Four pitfalls that hinder decision making

The path to prosperity, like any path, has many potential pitfalls along the way. I'll give you a list of traps to avoid when you're facing decisions that could affect your financial future. These traps can cause you to make bad decisions that risk derailing you from your path. Learn to avoid these obstacles and you'll find you make the right decisions more often.

The number one pitfall is procrastination. We're all guilty of it. When we face something we don't like, we put it off, saying,

'We'll cross that bridge when we get to it' or, 'We need to do a bit more research on that.' This kind of decision leads to analysis paralysis. It may be the easiest route to take, but it's usually the wrong one. Don't be a procrastinator and run from decisions. A procrastinator doesn't prosper. Remember, your decisions don't always have to be the right ones. You just have to grit your teeth and make them all the same. When I hear people say, 'I just wish something would happen in my life!' I think, *Well get moving!* Some people are so obsessed with making good decisions that they end up making no decisions at all. The longer you sit on your backside not making a decision, the harder it will be to break the deadlock and actually make a decision.

Some people allow their businesses to go under simply because they won't deal with an issue in their team. Some are willing to sacrifice the future of their business because they don't want to fire an employee who is holding the business back and eating away at their energy, their emotions and their capacity to move forward. They can see their business going down the gurgler and yet they keep that person where they are. Don't delay the inevitable. A vital recruitment policy is to hire slowly and fire quickly.

> If you wait for all the ducks to line up, you'll miss out on opportunities to progress.

The next decision-making trap is to hide behind information. Sometimes we delay a decision so we can search for all the available data. 'Oh I'm just waiting for everything to fall into place,' they say. If you wait for all the ducks to line up, you'll miss out on opportunities to progress. Those who demand perfect clarity rarely make a decision.

Another trap is to say yes to everything. I have found that if you are unsure about a decision, it's better to say no than yes. Why? Because it's easier later to change a no into a yes than to change a yes into a no. When people try to insist on an immediate answer, I say, 'If you force me to make a decision right now, then the answer is no, but if you give me more time to think about it, I might just be able to help.' To follow the path to prosperity, sometimes you have to learn to say 'no' more than 'yes', and for some people that's hard.

A further trap is to ignore feedback. If you have good people around you, ask them for their advice... and then listen. Allow others input into your decisions. If you ask for feedback, don't shoot the messenger when you don't like what they tell you. Appreciate feedback, as long as it's constructive and not destructive. The trick is to ask the *right* person the *right* question.

The most important facility you have is the ability to make decisions. Your decisions today can determine your destiny tomorrow. In the game of wealth, if you're going to be successful you have to learn to make decisions.

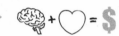

Take steps now to make better decisions

Write a list of the decisions you're facing right now that may have an impact on you financially. Then look at those decisions and ask yourself, *What major decisions and what minor decisions do I have to make today?* List them separately. With this list you will be better informed and better prepared to make the right decisions.

Major decisions I have to make now:

_____

_____

Minor decisions I have to make now:

_____

_____

Chapter 5

Are you a winner or a quitter?

Stay the course (once you're on the right path)

I hope by now you have made two vital decisions. First, you have decided on your financial goals, the reality you want to reach in time. This is your dream. It's what you need to focus your energy on. Second, you have made the decision to stay on the path towards that destination. It's very important that you make the commitment to stick to the path ahead. If you don't, your dream will be short-lived, and you will soon find yourself back where you are today. Once you have found the right path towards your destination, staying on it is critical... but often extremely difficult.

Dr Judah Folkman dreamed of discovering a cure for cancer. His field of research was angiogenesis, the growth of new blood vessels. In the early 1970s he proposed to the cancer research community that if tumors could be prevented from generating their own blood vessels they would die. But he was ridiculed for this idea, because it did not fit what scientists 'knew' to be true at that time. 'You're studying dirt,' they told him, meaning his project was futile science. But he was convinced he was right.

For two decades, despite the indifference and even hostility of colleagues, he persevered with his work. At one research convention where he spoke, half the audience walked out. 'He's only a surgeon,' he heard someone say. But he believed in his dream and he stuck to his path towards that dream. He was convinced that his work would one day help stop the growth of tumors. Then in the 1980s he and his colleagues made a breakthrough: they discovered the first angiogenesis inhibitors. The research community was shocked. It dawned on them that the man they had once ridiculed could no longer be ignored. Today more than 100 000 cancer patients are benefiting from the research he pioneered. His work is now recognised as being at the forefront of the fight against cancer.

Dr Folkman keeps a reproduction of a 1903 *New York Times* article in his archives. In it two physics professors explain why airplanes could not possibly fly. The article appeared just three months before the Wright brothers flew the first aircraft in human history at Kitty Hawk, North Carolina. 'There is a fine line between persistence and obstinacy,' Folkman says. 'I have come to realise the key is to choose a problem that is worth persistent effort.'

Your dream may require some fight

The things we obtain too cheaply we esteem too lightly.

Like Dr Judah Folkman, you and I may have to fight for our dream, but sometimes we give up way too easily. The things we obtain too cheaply we esteem too lightly. Often if we haven't struggled for something, we don't care too much if we lose it, but it's harder to give up what we have fought long and hard for. I want to give you the tools to help you to persevere — to grit your teeth, keep your eyes on the road ahead and continue taking one deliberate step after another in the right direction. Remember, it's direction, not intention, that takes you to your destination.

One of the greatest obstacles in your path is failure. If anyone knew about failure, it was Winston Churchill. In August 1929,

Churchill invested nearly $70000 in American stock and wrote a note to his wife saying how pleased he was to have reached a place of financial independence. Ninety days later the stock market collapsed and he lost virtually everything. Two years later, in 1931, after serving much of his career as a central figure in the British government, Churchill was denied a Cabinet post. While Adolf Hitler was building his war machine, Churchill, the only leading British politician who recognised the danger of the tyrant, was put out to pasture, banished to the political wilderness.

That same year, while trying to hold things together financially and fending off depression after his political defeat, Churchill made a tour of Canada and the United States. In New York City he looked the wrong way before crossing the street and was hit by a taxi travelling at 35 miles an hour. He was rushed to hospital, where his life hung by a thread. Churchill was 57 years old and in three years had been devastated by three life-shattering experiences. He had also been held responsible for a number of military defeats and faced a no-confidence motion in the British Parliament. His social plans for Great Britain were dismissed as extremist and widely ridiculed.

At the age of 65 Churchill was elected Prime Minister of Great Britain. As we all know, he went on to become one of Britain's — and the world's — greatest war leaders. He once said, 'Success consists of going from failure to failure without loss of enthusiasm.' He also said, 'Success is not final, failure is not fatal; it is the courage to continue that counts.'

Everyone fails — not just you. Understanding failure is one of the greatest tools to building prosperity. Failure should never kill your dream. In fact, failure can be used to increase your capacity for wealth.

'Colonel' Harland Sanders failed many times over before he built the successful KFC chain. He was fired from a dozen jobs before starting his first restaurant. He lost money in that business and found himself broke at the age of 65. But he didn't let it kill his dream.

Use failure as a springboard to success

All the most successful men and women in history have encountered failure—some many times—but used the experience as a springboard to success. American writer and self-improvement guru Dale Carnegie once said, 'Develop success from failures. Discouragement and failure are two of the surest stepping stones to success.' Theodore Roosevelt, the 26th US president, famously said:

> Far better is it to dare mighty things, to win glorious triumphs, even though checkered by failure...than to rank with those poor spirits who neither enjoy nor suffer much, because they live in a gray twilight that knows not victory nor defeat.

I too have failed many times. One of my greatest failures took place in 2001. Until that point my professional career had soared. I had sold more than half a million copies of my four books and was in the middle of writing my fifth. I was presenting a national weekly television program. I had sold hundreds of thousands of my own audio tapes and CDs. I was being booked as a corporate speaker a year in advance and was speaking to audiences totalling more than 300 000 a year all over the world. I was the director of one of Australia's most successful residential drug and alcohol rehabilitation centres. I had pioneered one of Australia's largest youth organisations and had helped build one of the world's greatest churches in Sydney.

In October that year I was in the United States on a speaking tour when a phone call home to Australia changed my life. I had made a mistake—of a personal nature. It began to dawn on me that this was an error that could potentially destroy my career, end friendships and—worst of all—break up my family. That night in my hotel room I couldn't sleep. I couldn't see the purpose of facing the next day, or the day after that. I thought my life was over.

Over the next few days, my world came crashing down around me. Through a series of phone calls and meetings I saw my life plummet from success mode to frantic mode. I was in the middle of a nightmare from which I couldn't wake up.

The upshot was that my marriage ended, my business folded, many friendships were tested and my sources of income dried up. One day I was standing before a crowd of 80 000 people; a week later I was revealed as a failure to some of my closest friends and family. Within a week, the Australian media began labelling me a failure. The story made the headlines in Australian newspapers and TV news reports. Radio talkback programs discussed it. My closest friends and family began telling me, 'It's over, Pat.' I felt the shame suffocating me, crushing every ounce of self-esteem I'd once had.

What do you do when you lose everything, when even your friends dump you? If you were an artist, it would be as if your brushes, paint and canvas were taken from you. What do you do when deep depression sets in? I'll tell you what you to do: you begin again, taking steps in a new direction. When everything changes, your only option is to change too. Some change is forced on you, some is a result of your own stupidity, but the bottom line is that if change is inevitable, then change it is.

So believe me when I say that I know from personal experience what it's like to fail. But through it all I've come to know one thing: you *can* make it through to the other side. Failure does not need to be the final chapter in your story. The good news is that, like so many others before me, I've emerged from the rubble. I've rebuilt my life, my career and my prosperity. I've got back on the right path.

We all make mistakes. But I've come to realise that in the long run it is not the failure itself that counts. What matters is to get back up, because it's much easier to stay down than to get back up. So don't let your failures stop you in your tracks. Don't let your failures destroy your dream and derail you from your path. Get right back up, because you've got to keep your dream alive.

Fight for your dream

Sometimes you have to fight for your dream. Whatever you do, don't give up one moment, one second or one event earlier than you should. You're the only one who can fulfil your destiny. It's the easiest thing in the world to find someone else to give you your dream or to tell you why you can't achieve your dream. You may have been told all your life that you can't. Your husband, wife, father, brother or teacher may have poured cold water on your dream. Maybe today no-one believes in you. Well that stops right now, because I want to tell you that I believe in you. Why? Because you've picked up this book, and the fact that you're reading this book tells me that you hunger to succeed and, more importantly, that you are prepared to invest in your success. But that won't make any difference in the world unless you believe in yourself. If *you* don't believe in yourself, you will never succeed. The only thing that can stop you is your own internal DNA.

Don't quit your dream. I have found that quitting is more about *who* you are than *where* you are in life. 'Winners never quit and quitters never win.' Somehow we think that people who fulfil their dreams have had an easier road to success than the rest of us. But the truth is that most successful people have lived one hell of a life! The difference is that when knocked down they kept getting back up and trying again. They kept believing in themselves.

In each one of us there is a lower self and a higher self fighting for our attention.

The lower self says, *Not enough people believe in me — I'll never make it.*

The higher self says, *My belief in me is enough — I can make it.*

The lower self says, *It's taking too long to realise my dream.*

The higher self says, *Dreams are realised one day at a time.*

The lower self says, *Enough is enough — I can't take it any more!*

The higher self says, *I've come too far to quit now.*

The lower self says, *I don't have enough strength to hold onto my dream.*

The higher self says, *I'll hold on a little longer — the darkest hour is just before the dawn.*

Which self do you listen to most? Does your higher self prosper or do you allow your lower self to control your circumstances?

Can't people and can people

There are two types of people in this world — *can't* people and *can* people.

The can't person says, *We've never done that before.*

The can person says, *We have an opportunity to be the first.*

The can't person says, *We don't have enough resources.*

The can person says, *Necessity fuels invention.*

The can't person says, *There's not enough time.*

The can person says, *Well let's change how we work and find the time.*

The can't person says, *We've already tried that.*

The can person asks, *What have we learned from that?*

The can't person says, *It's a waste of time.*

The can person says, *Think of the possibilities!*

The can't person says, *Our vendors won't go for it.*

The can person says, *Let's present them with another opportunity.*

The can't person says, *We don't have enough money.*

The can person says, *There is some way we can cut a deal and make it happen.*

The can't person says, *Our situation will never get any better!*

The can person says, *Let's see how we can find a way to make things better.*

When I started the Australian youth organisation Youth Alive, they warned me it had never been done before. I said, 'Fantastic! I'm a pioneer!' When I took over the financially struggling drug rehabilitation centre, they warned me, 'A successful drug rehab centre has never been run before!' I said, 'No problem! I'll be the first to do it!' Today I enjoy being Australia's first prosperity activist. Why am I an 'activist'? Because an activist is someone who fights for someone else's rights—*yours*. You have a right to prosper no matter what your circumstances or background or disadvantages. Your decisions, not your circumstances, will determine you prosperity.

> Your decisions, not your circumstances, will determine your prosperity.

Which side of the fence are you on? Are you a *can't* person or a *can* person? Because that will make all the difference in your journey to a prosperous life.

Distractions take you off course

When I was a teenager my cousin was a professional boxer. He was my hero. He looked sharp. He was sporty and incredibly muscular. I thought to myself, *That's what I want to be!* So I followed in my cousin's footsteps and began to climb up the ladder of amateur boxing.

One night I came up against a good-looking, blond guy who had a gorgeous girlfriend. As I listened to my coach in the dressing room, I knew I could take him out. He had the fancy footwork and the ripped muscles, but I knew the one thing he didn't have was my tenacity. When we entered the ring I noticed his gorgeous girlfriend ringside. I thought, *Man, you are going down in front of this girl! I am going to show up, show off and take you out!*

Well, the first round went pretty well for me. I kept hitting him, but he kept coming back. The second round came and went and I figured I was way ahead on points, but in the third round I discovered his secret weapon. As I was about to give him one of my fatal blows, out of the corner of my eye I noticed his girlfriend, looking at me with her gorgeous blue eyes, and she winked at me. Well, that's all I remember of the fight. That was the day I fell to a fatal distraction.

Remember the 1987 movie *Fatal Attraction*, starring Michael Douglas and Glenn Close? A happily married New York lawyer has a brief affair with a work colleague, but the problem escalates when she reveals she wants much more than that. She will stop at nothing to have him all to herself. Dan Callagher (Michael Douglas) is on a pathway to prosperity with his wife and family, but one fatal attraction — or one fatal *distraction* — ruins his life. What fatal distraction has the potential to take you off your pathway? You see, your attention determines your direction. What captures your attention influences your direction towards your destination. That's the principle of the path in three words: *attention, direction* and *destination*. As your attention goes, so goes your life. What captures your focus will capture your future. The wise king Solomon said, 'Let your eyes look straight ahead, fix your gaze directly before you.' His father, David, said: 'Turn my eyes away from worthless things.' Both Solomon and David were alluding to the immense power our attention has over our life. We need to avoid fatal distractions, whether in our relationships, our career, our business or our finances.

How many famous sportspeople have been derailed by fatal distractions? The list is a mile long. No-one will forget Tiger Woods' fall from grace in 2009. Boxer Mike Tyson had many distractions throughout his professional life. Basketballer Kobe Bryant is another sports star whose career was impacted by a sexual encounter. How many businesspeople and politicians are you aware of who allowed fatal distractions to damage their financial world? It may have been a wrong relationship, an addiction or the giddy attraction of power itself that brought them down. We shake our heads in disbelief, but to err is human and to rebuild takes guts. It's the principle, not the degree, I am highlighting here. We all suffer financial, and even moral, highs and lows, but if we focus only on what's not working or what we have done wrong, that's all we'll ever have. Change requires focus.

So what about you? What or who has your attention? Has anything or anyone so captured your attention as to derail you from your path? Be honest. It could be a new relationship, a new business opportunity or a persistent addiction to something you know is wrong. Let me ask the same question in a different way: is there something or someone that you need to begin paying *more* attention to? Should you be paying more attention to your budget, your close personal and professional relationships, or your physical, emotional and spiritual health? Should you be doing more training in the area of your products or in business generally? This is important because distractions can steal your time and rob you of what's most important to your financial success.

What does a distraction do? It puts distance between you and your goal. Often the easiest thing to do is the very thing you *shouldn't* do. For example, you know you're supposed to be closing a business deal and instead you meet with a friend of a friend to give them some personal advice. Could that time have been put to better use?

Distractions interrupt progress

Distractions interrupt your progress. One of the keys to prosperity is the ability to build momentum towards your financial goals in your business or organisation. Distractions very quickly interrupt that momentum and cause you to stray from your desired destination. They can also attract negativity and make you consume energy in unproductive activities, wasting valuable time. It helps to monitor your energy reserves constantly. If your tank is running low because you expended effort in the wrong activity, you will have no energy left to achieve your real goal.

Distractions leave you time poor. They take you off course and before long you realise your wasted time cannot be redeemed. They are time-sucking bugs and they are everywhere. No-one is immune. We have only 24 hours in a day, so let's make sure we use them well.

A distracted person is a nuisance to everyone else too. He is the guy who regularly turns up at your office door and asks, 'Want to go for a coffee?' Or the woman who starts a project for you but then finds 35 other tasks to do at the same time. These people waste not only their own valuable time but yours too. And time is money, so avoid them.

How do you overcome distractions? First, ask yourself this all-important question every morning when you start your day, *What do I need to do today?* Notice the word *need*? I didn't say *want*. Your wants are a distraction from your needs. Plan your day by making a list of the tasks you still need to attend to, distinguishing those that are *important* from those that are *urgent*. There is a big difference. Important means 'significant and of consequence', whereas urgent means 'requiring immediate action or attention'. We can get caught up in immediate, urgent things while neglecting the more significant, important things. If you neglect the important tasks, they will soon become bigger and more urgent than ever.

> If you neglect the important tasks, they will soon become...more urgent than ever.

Second, if you don't get everything done today, don't beat yourself up for getting distracted. If you didn't do everything you needed to do yesterday, don't waste time worrying about it. Simply return to where you stopped yesterday and place the task somewhere on today's list.

Third, sometimes you need to overcome yourself. By this I mean that your biggest distraction is not other people, it's *you*! Learn to focus. Become more disciplined. Invest in your learning, and learn to use your time wisely. Apply yourself to improve in this area and you will become much more productive in your journey towards a prosperous future.

Fourth, overcome distractions by understanding your goals and your dream. Your dream has got to be clear, because only then can it become a priority. We never prioritise something that's fuzzy. Clarity burns bright and holds our attention.

Finally, take regular breaks. Time out refreshes the mind, body and spirit—we all need it. It is important that you take a break when you're tired because exhaustion can be a huge distraction.

Where your focus is today, your future is tomorrow

Remember: where your focus is today, your future is tomorrow. Focus is a discipline that needs to be developed. To stay on course, you need to learn how to keep your mind focused. Your mind is like a muscle. Just as regular exercise and physical exertion build and strengthen your muscles, your mind is strengthened by focus. If you want to see increased progress in any area of your life, keep your focus on your goals and don't allow distractions to rule you. Successful people know how to keep their focus firmly and clearly on their desired ends.

Focus is made up of five key factors:

Forward planning

Overcoming distractions

Committing to a plan

Understanding your objectives

Sustaining effort.

Create an environment for focus in your life. Your mind will function better if you create the right environment for it. It's your responsibility to create the environment you desire — whether for your business, your home or your relationships. The environment you create for your mind will determine your success. Eliminating or learning to ignore distractions is part of this process.

Prosperity has to be actively pursued. That's what focus is all about — relentless pursuit. In his book *Focus — The Future of Your Company Depends on It*, Al Ries offers a great illustration of the difference between focus and lack of focus. He describes how the sun is a powerful source of energy. Every hour the sun washes the Earth with billions of kilowatts of energy. Yet with a hat and some sunscreen, you can bathe in the light of the sun for hours at a time with few ill effects. A laser, on the other hand, is a weak source of energy, yet focusing a few watts of energy in a fine stream of light will cut through steel in a moment. That's the power of focus. Unleash the power of focused thinking and you will reap the rewards.

Take steps now to stay on track

Write down three distractions that have the potential to derail your plans for financial success:

1 _____

2 _____

3 _____

Next to each distraction listed, write down how you are going to overcome it. It may be through training, meditation or a daily plan of action, for example.

If you want prosperity in your life, start focusing now. Discipline your mind. Recognise distractions and resist them. Your mind is your greatest asset. Give it plenty of attention. Feed it with great books, positive audio CDs and successful environments. Whenever you are in your car, listen to successful people as they teach you the principles and attitudes of success. If you want more assets, a higher income or a larger business, then you have to learn to think in a certain way. So make a decision today to start focusing!

Chapter 6

What laws do you live by?
The irrefutable rules of money

As you probably realise, I'm Italian, and Italians are fairly proficient at football (or soccer, as it's known in some parts of the world). I'll never forget the time I played my first game. As I laced up my boots I thought to myself, *How hard can this be? I watch Italians play this game all the time. It should come naturally to me. After all, many of the greatest football players — and some of the highest paid sports stars in the world — are Italian. I can probably make my fortune playing football too!*

It might help to know that I was one of those teenagers who didn't bother to learn the rules. I thought all I had to do was kick the round ball into the rectangular goal at the opposite end of the field. I ran onto the pitch and began chasing that bouncing ball all over the park. And the referee kept following me wherever I ran, blowing his little whistle until he was red in the face. He kept stopping the game and pointing at me. *What a party-pooper!* I thought. *What a killjoy!*

How was I to know I couldn't kick a player's legs when he didn't give me the ball? No-one told me I couldn't stand in the opposition's goal mouth waiting for the ball so I could kick it straight in. I didn't know that when you throw the ball into the field of play you have to do it over your head. I didn't even realise that otherwise only the goalkeeper can touch the ball with his hands. I just figured I could play the game my own way. After all, I'm Italian. Boy, did I learn the hard way!

Have you ever played a game and not known the rules? If played against others who knew the rules, you didn't stand a chance! So why do we expect to win in the game of money if we don't take the trouble to learn the rules? In most areas of life there are rules, principles or laws that govern success. If we don't know them, we're unlikely to succeed. They govern how we participate in the game in institutions, in society and in life generally.

> I may have failed the laws [of prosperity] many times, but they have never failed me.

In this chapter I am going to introduce you to the laws of prosperity that the wealthy know. These laws will change your life — if you apply them effectively. I may have failed these laws many times, but they have never failed me.

The time-honoured laws of money

Most people think they can break the time-honoured laws of money and still prosper. It's like telling me that you can drive down a road doing 130 kilometres an hour in a 100 km/h zone and not break a traffic law or risk causing an accident. Only idiots do that. There are consequences to your actions. If you break the law, you pay the price. If you don't like the laws, well then you are welcome to go and live on your own planet. You don't have to believe in these laws for them to work. They operate whether you believe in them or not. All laws operate that way. For example, you may tell me you don't believe in the law of gravity, but I will guarantee you that if you jump off the roof you'll injure yourself.

Some time ago I was invited to speak at a big convention in the US. I arrived early that day to check out the facility, and as my guides showed me around the 16 000-seat arena, they pointed out a special stage that extended out into the audience. It had been left that way from a function held the previous evening. I looked at that stage and thought to myself, *This is going to be fun!*

When I went back to the arena that night, I was so excited. I was dressed in my best suit and had prepared a message that would blow their socks off. The organisers greeted me and took me via a back entrance onto the stage, where the MC introduced me to the crowd. I ran onto the stage and launched straight into my message. I was hot! I was on fire! I held the audience in the palm of my hand. I had them clapping and cheering. Then I decided it was time to take it to another level, so I strode confidently out into the audience to deliver my main point of the evening. One second I was walking across the stage before 16 000 people and the next second I'd disappeared. I found myself sprawled awkwardly on a cold, hard floor. In the rush of my arrival, the organisers forgot to tell me they had retracted the part of the stage that extended out into the audience. In a split second I was back up on that stage finishing my main point, still wondering what had just happened, but I just kept going.

I've fallen off stages a few times since then. I'm getting used to it. But if there's one thing I have learned, it's this: you never mess with the law of gravity! Whether you accept the law of gravity or not, the fact is that this force existed before the apple fell on Newton's head ... and before I fell off that stage. In the same way, the laws of money have existed almost as long as time itself. Now I am going to unravel the 12 laws of money that have the potential to pull you out of poverty. Applied on a regular basis, each has the potential to increase your wealth beyond your dreams. They are the keys that will unlock what has been missing in your life so far. If you practise these principles, you will profit from the principles you practise. The wealthy save money and spend what's left; the broke spend their money and invest what's left, which is generally zero. Here they are:

1 The Law of Stretching

I also call this one *the principle of pulling back*. If you want an arrow to go the distance, you've got to pull it back on your bow as far as you can. The further back you pull, the further it will travel. In your own life, the more you stretch yourself, the more you will expand your capacity for wealth.

Stretching is great for your financial health. I run wealth creation events in Australia and globally to stretch people because I know it will expand their wealth potential. We flourish in an environment where we are surrounded by people who, like us, are passionately pursuing prosperity, because it stretches us to see and believe that more wealth is possible.

The greatest momentum you will ever achieve is in pulling back. Some people complain, 'Oh I can't afford to attend financial seminars like that!' or, 'I don't have the time. I'm too busy.' Listen, some of the busiest people in the world attend my events. It's all a matter of priorities, better time management and budgeting.

Your business *can* grow. You *can* enjoy a prosperous life. You *can* increase your financial capacity. But for that to happen you need to stretch your dreams, your imagination, your creativity and your mindset. Stretching hurts, but it expands your ability to make money. Stretching involves placing yourself in a position that isn't comfortable, like joining a club or association where you are forced to rub shoulders with high achievers and wealthy people. Stretching involves mixing with people who are going to help you get where you want to go.

There is something different about the wealthy: the way they think, the way they make decisions, the way they network. The experiences that got you where you are now financially will not take you where you want to go. It's going to take a whole new level of stretching to reach your financial destination.

2 The Law of Vision

I talked about this law in chapter 2. Vision means clearly imagining your goals as if you have already achieved them. It's important to list where we want to go, what we want to do and with whom we want to do it. If you do not know what you want, no-one can help you get it. In her book *First Steps to Wealth*, Dani Johnson writes, 'If you want to be successful financially, expand your income to fit your dreams.'

We should never live life in a hit-and-miss way. We need a vision for life. If we don't have one, someone else will. Vision is a powerful thing. It sets direction. People without a clear vision are easily distracted. They drift from one activity to another, one relationship to another, one business to another. Instead, set your course, set your direction and pursue your vision. When we have a vision we are consumed by what is and what could be. Perhaps your vision is to build a better financial base for your family or to feed people in need.

All visions begin with passion. What are you passionate about? I'm passionate about prosperity. I'm passionate about giving people positive, inspiring, life-changing experiences, about stretching people so they can live beyond and above the normality of their current life. Your passion should lead and feed your vision.

3 The Law of the Mind

Education begins in your mind. It is important to learn first and earn second. You can learn by accessing the gift of prior learning—the wisdom of others. How do you think? Are you racked by worry and doubt or are you hopeful about your future? Can you see the possibilities in everything? Before you can build wealth you need to think like a wealthy person. The first place change needs to happen is in your mind. You need to shift your thinking from a poverty mindset to a prosperity mindset. We all need the right kind of mindset to achieve wealth and prosperity. Change your mindset and you'll change your destiny.

The problem with a lot of us is that we have a virus in our mind that stops us from moving to higher financial levels. Just as desktop computers require virus protection, our minds also need virus protection. Don't allow mindset viruses to infiltrate. It's vital that you learn how to eradicate them instantly.

You can't have a million-dollar income with a five-dollar mindset.

We need to be able to change our mindset to think consistently the way wealthy people think. We can do that by educating ourselves in areas that need growth. Read books about wealth. Listen to inspiring audio messages about millionaire mindsets. Watch video programs that stretch your financial capacity. The bottom line is that your income won't keep you where your mindset can't hold you. You can't have a million-dollar income with a five-dollar mindset.

Are you willing to get rid of the thought patterns, ideas about yourself and your world, and mindsets about money and wealth that have kept you contained and prevented you from stepping into the truly prosperous life that you were born for and that is waiting to be discovered? In chapter 8 I will show you how to develop the right mindset for a prosperous life.

4 The Law of Value

People pay you according to your perceived value. What determines your value? Mostly it's your skill set. So if you increase your skills, you will increase your value and that will increase your income. But here's a tip: don't spread yourself too thin. You can't be good at everything. If you want your life to be a success, it is important to focus on the one thing that your life can be given to. Find your place in the world and stick to it.

One of the mistakes I made years ago was to spread myself too thin. I began doing too much. I was running six organisations and sitting on the boards of several other worthwhile causes. My intentions were good, but I was diluting my strengths and my focus to the point that I was no longer fully effective.

Most of the world's great achievers were great at one thing. Mother Teresa didn't feed everyone or run programs for every needy person in Calcutta. She targeted a specific group. You can't be the best at everything. People who think they are good at everything generally are expert at nothing. So learn to add value by focusing on specific key strengths.

5 The Law of the Seed

Some people call this the Law of Seedtime and Harvest or the Law of Investment and Return. I believe this is the greatest of all the laws. The bottom line is that we reap what we sow. Whatever we give or invest in will grow and we will receive a reward down the track. A farmer knows that if he sows seeds in fertile soil in the right season, he will reap a harvest within a given time frame. This time-honoured law applies to every area of our lives — even our finances. And it can work for you if you will apply it. This is such an important law that I have dedicated chapter 7 to it.

6 The Law of Teachability

What you know has brought you to where you are right now. But you need more knowledge and wisdom to progress further towards your dream. So how do you get it? Through education, through a commitment to personal development, and through mentors who will challenge you and teach you things you would not otherwise learn. Other steps to learning include reading, being inquisitive and asking questions, and employing a coach. If you want to prosper, then follow what successful people do and say. If they tell you to read a book about managing your money, do it. Show me a person who is committed to their personal development and I will show you a person who will add value to themselves, to their clients and to their businesses.

I have had to learn a lot in order to become more effective in my life. I have learned to work smarter, not harder. I have learned to shift from being a driven person to being a leading person. I have learned how to change the way I approach life. I have seen too many people with big visions held back by their pride. They were not teachable, were unwilling to lend an ear to advice. They thought they knew everything so they stopped learning. And sadly, their potential for wealth diminished as a result.

You don't know what you don't know — no-one does — but the fact that you are reading this book tells me that you have a spirit of teachability. Don't let it die. Remember, education is not expensive; ignorance is.

7 The Law of Forgiveness

When you do not forgive, you make decisions out of bitterness. Mahatma Gandhi said, 'The weak can never forgive. Forgiveness is the attitude of the strong.' When people have ripped you off in a business deal, when people have hurt you, it takes strength to forgive them. Sure, you can never forget things. You are not a computer that can erase its memory bank, but you must forgive. You can expend your energy blaming others for things that go wrong in your life, for your lack of success or your financial woes. Or you can choose to forgive others when they have wronged you. Forgiveness is your choice.

Have you been mistreated and vowed never to forget the abuse as long as you live? Whether you know it or not, the unforgiveness you are harbouring is a sign of weakness. Don't be a carrier of that disease. It also takes strength to forgive yourself. Refusing to forgive yourself and to move on in life is an act of cowardice.

Forgiveness is a bridge that every single one of us has to cross. There is nothing that has ever happened to you or to anyone else that cannot be forgiven. In spite of the indignities that he suffered through 27 years of prison life, Nelson Mandela showed no hint of bitterness towards his former jailers, exemplifying instead a life of dignity and understanding with all people. Your heart's memory must eliminate the bad things and magnify the good. We must always be thankful that in spite of what others do to us or what we may have done to others, there is still hope in the future. Forgiveness cleans the decks of our lives. Resentment and anger always hurts *us* more than the person we refuse to forgive.

I remember during one of my periods of rebuilding how a friend challenged me about how bitter I was becoming. I immediately defended myself, but in my reply I heard exactly what she had heard and I realised what I was becoming. I had to uproot bitterness from my life or it would have become a tree that would bear ugly fruit, not just in *my* life, but in my children's lives and possibly in the lives of my friends and colleagues. I refuse to get bitter and I choose to forgive. Learning to forgive ourselves and others helps us soar into a positive future, and it builds a platform for greater wealth and prosperity. In business, too, forgive and move on. Don't think about getting even. Get on top and get going.

8 The Law of Promotion

There's an ancient proverb that says, 'If you are faithful with little, you will end up with much.' In the same way, if you are not faithful with the little, you are never going to get the much. If you want more than you have, then value and take better care of what you have now. If you can't look after a $30 pair of shoes, what makes you think you can look after a $300 pair? If you can't clean your hunk-o-junk car every week, what makes you think you could look after a Mercedes?

Dani Johnson offers this advice:

> Prosper where you are planted. Work with what you have. If you have a job that you might think is 'little', be the best at it, affect people there, make a difference wherever you are. The road to success is often paved with things we do not want to do.

Some people call this the Law of Faithfulness with Small Things. It means that if we can be faithful with our time, money or influence, then we will be given more. Do you want more influence? Then take care of the small amount you currently have. If you have two minor, unimportant customers now, be thankful and treat them as if they were the last two customers on the planet. Remember, it's the little things that make the difference.

So what do you have that is unique? What little do you have that you can turn into something? Sometimes, while we wait for the big break, the little opportunities that can open the door pass us by. Focus on what you have, not on what you don't have.

Rick Hoyt has cerebral palsy. When he was born the doctors warned his parents that he would never be anything more than a 'vegetable', but they were determined to raise him like any other child. When he turned 10, Rick's life changed dramatically. Engineers at Tufts University created a device that enabled him to communicate via a computer. He painstakingly typed out his first words: 'Go Bruins!' That's when everyone discovered he was a sports fan.

> Sometimes, while we wait for the big break, the little opportunities... pass us by.

After many trials Rick entered the public school system, where he excelled. Two years later, he found out about a five kilometre fundraising run to help a young athlete paralysed in an accident. He told his father he wanted to participate. His dad agreed to run and push his son in a modified wheelchair. They crossed the finishing line second to last, but that day Team Hoyt was born. They acquired a more sophisticated chair and the quadriplegic teenager and his out-of-shape dad began running together. In 1981 they ran their first Boston Marathon. Since then they have not missed one in 20 years. Rick has since earned his degree and works at Boston University helping design computer systems for people with disabilities. As of November 2011, the Hoyts had competed in 1069 endurance events, including 69 marathons and six Ironman triathlons.

Sometimes we complain about what we don't have and don't realise the treasure that is within our grasp. If we could only explore what we have already been given!

9 The Law of Focus

It is amazing how things can happen that could be avoided if only we paid attention. The great lesson of life is what you feed or focus on grows but what you starve dies. Some years ago I built a new home and decided to plant beautiful flowers and trees in my yard. A green thumb was never one of my strengths, but I thought I'd have a go. A year later, talking with some friends, I mentioned how the plants were not doing well and that I thought the soil was not as good as at home where I grew up. 'So, Pat,' one of my friends joked, 'have you tried watering them?' But she was right! I had wanted the plants to grow, but I had not given them the attention they needed.

We must pay attention to the things that help us build our lives successfully. You can't ignore things and hope they'll get better. You can't ignore your business and expect it to grow. What you focus on will progress; what you neglect will regress. The investments you pay attention to will reward you; those you neglect will not. Instead, they may cause you a lot of financial harm. Understand that many of the things that happen to us occur not because of fate or bad luck, but because we did not pay attention.

Focus on the things that are important to you. What aspects of your life are being neglected and starved? Negligence requires no effort, whereas attention and focus require great effort.

10 The Law of Honour

Dani Johnson writes, 'It's about honoring people and giving them what they want. When you honor people, they honor you back, but it is not always the one you honor who honors you back.' Often it's as simple as smiling at someone. A kind word of encouragement works like magic. Look people in the eye, address them by name and talk about what they are passionate about. Genuinely honouring others is a skill, and skills can be learned. Everyone wants to feel special and important, including you. Always make time for the people who enter your life every day.

Charles Plumb was a US navy pilot in Vietnam. After 75 missions his plane was destroyed and he parachuted into enemy territory. He survived six years in a Communist prison and now he lectures on his experiences. One day a stranger came up to him and said, 'Your name is Plumb. You flew fighter jets from the aircraft carrier *Kitty Hawk* and you got shot down.' Plumb asked the man how he knew those things about him. Smiling, the stranger said, 'I packed your parachute. I guess it worked.'

That night Plumb could not sleep. He kept wondering what the man had looked like in uniform and how many times he had walked right past this ordinary seaman without noticing him. Plumb thought about the hours the man spent in the bow of the ship weaving the shrouds and folding the silks of each chute—holding in his hands the fate of someone he didn't even know.

Make sure you notice people. Go out of your way to pay attention to people who do things for you—people who ask you questions, who shake your hand, who greet you and who serve you. Don't make the mistake of not enjoying the experience of others. People—not the internet, not the market, not some mystical belief, but people—bring you money. Honour them, do the right thing by them, and you will be rewarded.

11 The Law of Decision

I dedicated chapter 4 to this very important law. Generally, prosperity does not happen by accident. To become prosperous you need to make the decision to become prosperous and then to decide how you are going to do so. It takes a decision on your part, and then it takes a series of ongoing decisions to build wealth over the long term.

If you're not fully committed to becoming prosperous, then you can't blame anyone or anything else for your lack of prosperity. Your upbringing, your job, your organisation, your education—none of these are responsible for your prosperity. The only person that matters in your journey towards a prosperous life is *you*! You have to decide that you are going to be wealthy. So make a decision.

12 The Law of Action

The rewards of prosperity come from your actions, not your intentions. Have you ever met people who are always about to do something, but they never actually quite get there? People do not respect intentions — they respect action.

When we sit with indecision, says Dani Johnson, we invite our enemies — procrastination, fear, unbelief and excuses — into our lives. When we immediately follow up our decisions with action, a funnel of favour begins. Doors begin to open. People begin to help us. Our life's purpose becomes clear and our self-motivation mobilises us from the inside out. There's a saying: 'One good action is greater than a million good intentions.' We have to learn to be people of positive action, not professional procrastinators. I love this inspirational poem:

Did is a word of achievement

Won't is a word of retreat

Might is a word of bereavement

Can't is a word of defeat

Ought is a word of duty

Try is a word each hour

Will is a word of beauty

Can is a word of power.

Progress in life always involves action and risk. Action produces results. Every prosperous person you know is a person of action. These are people who passionately pursue their dream — through action.

Imagine walking into the garage and getting into the car. You sit at the wheel, steering this way and that. You don't turn on the ignition, so you aren't moving. Night after night you get into that car and move that wheel to the left and to the right. You're not moving forward, just sitting and steering. Surely your wife, your children and your friends would think you'd lost your mind!

So many people do this in life. They want to get ahead, to be successful, to make a lot of money. They want to be known for achieving great things...but they forget to turn on the ignition so as to get moving. They just think, *One day I'm gonna...One day I will...* If you want to get ahead you have to get moving. You can't steer a parked car. Too many people just spin their wheels. They burn a lot of rubber, make a lot of noise and blow a lot of smoke, but they're not going forward.

It's time to get your dream on the road. Don't keep it parked in the garage of disappointment, let-down, frustration and despair. Turn on the ignition, put the pedal to the metal to get moving and steer yourself towards a great destiny.

Take steps now to act on your dream

Take *action* now. Ask yourself this question:

What have I been procrastinating over? What actions that I have been avoiding do I need to take to get back on the path to prosperity? List them here:

1 _____

2 _____

3 _____

Now write down when you are going to start taking action in each of these areas. Write down the date and show your list to someone you trust, someone you become accountable to for doing what you have promised to do. No more excuses please!

What are you giving?
Your harvest is determined by your seed

When I took over the drug rehabilitation program in Sydney, people were donating secondhand fridges, beds, sheets, clothes and shoes. Some of the sheets had holes in them and many of the t-shirts were torn. I was mad. I said to my staff, 'If you don't want to wear those old clothes and shoes, what makes you think the boys will want to wear the ugly things!' Now, I appreciated those secondhand gifts, but I didn't appreciate the message they were sending to the young men in the program. So I instructed the staff that our first task was to clear out all the secondhand stuff.

'Okay, so how are we going to clothe the boys?' they asked.

'Not in those clothes!' I shot back.

'But where are we going to get the money to buy them new clothes and shoes and beds and sheets?' they asked.

So I wrote to clothing companies asking them to donate new clothes. A businessman who owned one of the largest clothing companies in the city had a son who was a drug addict. He contacted me and said, 'I'll give your boys clothes for the rest of their lives — just help my son!' As far as I know, that company is still sending new jeans and t-shirts to the rehab centre. Next I wrote to bed manufacturers to ask for 30 new beds. I told them I would be happy to put their business name in the centre's newsletter. We ended up with new beds, new sheets, new shoes — the best of everything.

My next project was a bus. The bus we had at that time was about to fall apart, but with the help of a generous sponsor we acquired a brand-new bus. Soon afterwards some of the boys came up to me and said, 'Pat, can you take those signs off the bus?'

'Why?' I asked.

'Because when we're on the bus, we don't want to advertise to people that we're in a drug rehab program. It's embarrassing for us. We're not addicts anymore!'

I agreed, so we removed the name from the sides of the bus. Every month we would drive that bus to a pizza parlor for dinner. One day I got all the young men together and said, 'Whoever achieves the best results in the gym this week gets to drive to the pizza parlour in my car.'

It's amazing what a bit of motivation can do, especially when it involves driving a brand-new Lexus! Those boys responded immediately. They lifted weights like never before. They broke personal records in days. A week later I stood before the boys. They all looked eager and pumped, and I saw something different in their eyes. I awarded the prize to James, who had been one of the worst rogues in the group. When the day arrived, I tossed the car keys to him and said, 'We'll see you at the pizza parlour.'

'You're letting me drive your car without you in it?' he asked.

'Yep.'

'Pat, have you seen my police record? Do you know what I was convicted for?'

'Car theft.'

'And you're going to get on the bus and let me drive off with your car on my own? What if I steal it?' he asked.

'It'll be the last thing you ever do in your life!' I replied.

'I thought so,' he responded. Then he hung his head and asked, 'Do you really trust me?'

I looked that young man in the eyes and said, 'Yes, James, I do. I trust you.'

Every investment brings a return

James ended up becoming one of our head students. In fact, he became one of the finest young men I've ever known. That was a magic moment in his life. Until then, everyone had labelled him a thief and a drug addict. No-one had placed trust in him. No-one had invested in him. The investment of trust produced a return of responsibility.

That day James grabbed the car keys and drove off. We met him at the pizza parlour half an hour later. All the boys wore their new t-shirts, jeans and shoes. As we were enjoying our pizza, a few local gang members walked in looking for trouble. They looked at my boys and picked on one of them. I watched as the boys got out their knives and began cleaning them.

'What are you doing?' I asked.

'We're getting ready to rumble,' they told me.

Then James stood up and said, 'We've got to be bigger than that, boys. The hardest fight to walk away from is the one you don't get into. Let's just go help clean up in the kitchen.'

I watched every one of them stand up and follow James into the kitchen. They approached the owner and said, 'We've got a choice to make. We can go out there and have a fight, or we can help you in here, sir. So what do you need done?'

That night they made an investment in that restaurant owner's business. They cleaned the kitchen and wiped down every table. The owner walked over to me and said, 'Who are these boys?'

I told him.

'They're drug addicts?' he asked.

'They were, but they're in recovery and changing their lives. They've been clean for a couple of months.'

'And they come and work in my kitchen?' he said, shaking his head. 'You've touched my heart. From now on, every time you boys come into my pizza place, you come for free.'

The greatest law of wealth creation

In that moment, this pizza owner acted on one of the greatest laws of wealth creation, and he probably didn't even realise it. It's called the Law of Investment and Return or the Law of Seedtime and Harvest, and I spoke of it in chapter 6. If you apply this law, it will absolutely change your life, even if you are not aware of how it works. If you understand the power of this law and apply it regularly, it will transform your finances, your relationships, your business and your career. It has the potential to be the greatest activator of wealth you will ever see. If you apply it and continue to apply it, it will bring about a massive increase in your life. It's such a simple law that many people tend to gloss over it or ignore it. But without this law nothing else can happen. It's one of those eternal laws that dates back to the beginning of time.

The ancients called it the Law of Seedtime and Harvest for a reason. The old parable tells the story of the farmer who sows his seed in good ground gaining a rich crop. *Sowing*, of course, is another word for *investing*, and seeds represent the things of value in your life. When you sow, you purposely give away or invest something valuable with an expectation that it will generate a return in the future.

Your seed could be your money, your skills, your time, your words — each has the capacity to bring increased value to someone else and to you. In the parable, the farmer sowed seed knowing that much of it would yield a crop. The miracle of this law is that your sowing will generate much more than you put in. That's what seeds do. A seed planted on fertile ground will sprout up and when it matures will generate fruit — and a lot more seed. Those seeds can then be planted again, generating an even bigger harvest. That's how the farmer in this story saw his seeds yield a crop that was up to a hundred times what he had actually invested. Wouldn't you like to see that kind of return on your investments!

What's your soil like?

Here is a great truth: soil must be prepared through labour. You've got to work the ground, pull out the weeds, enrich it, sometimes fertilise it. In the story, some of the farmer's seed fell in the wrong place: rather than soft, moist fertile soil, the ground was stony and hard. The soil represents your heart, your mindset, your attitudes and beliefs. For example, if you are angry or mistrustful, then you are not providing fertile soil for a life of prosperity. You've got negative issues that must be dug up and dealt with before your life can become more financially fruitful. In the next chapter I deal with these issues. Most of us have a mindset that in some way holds us back financially—sometimes big time!

Other seed was scattered widely across the soil and was eaten by birds, or it fell on thorny ground and the thorns choked the seedlings as they tried to grow. What do the birds and thorns represent today? They are the naysayers—the people who are always repeating the same old catch-cries, imploring us not to bother investing or showing generosity: 'Don't risk it!' they say. 'Just play it safe!' Or, 'Why are you always wanting to make more money? Why don't you just settle for what you've got?' Or, 'Hold on to your hard-earned money!' They are the people who try to choke the life out of you, to pull you down, to hold you back. 'You wasted your money on those personal development seminars!' Or, 'You spent how much? You could lose it all!'

> What you neglect will die but what you feed will grow.

Do you have people like that in your life? They steal your seeds away from you…because you let them. They rob you of a wealthy future because they don't allow your seed to take root and grow and produce a harvest. Learn to ignore them, because what you neglect will die but what you feed will grow.

In chapter 9 I talk about how the people we associate with influence our financial situation. Some of the people we hang around are content to have just enough money to get by. I've heard people say, 'I just need enough money to put food on the table, no more.' When you think about it, that's a selfish attitude. You and I should be able to earn enough money to put food on our own table *and someone else's table too*. Why be content with just enough money to look after your own limited needs? There are lots of people around you in greater need, and you can do something to help them. Dream bigger dreams, my friend. Don't let the thorns and the birds steal your potential for a life of prosperity. These types of people can so easily hold you back. Being around them is like driving with the handbrake on. They'll block you, choking off your chances of a prosperous future.

Don't eat your seed

Then there are other people who treat their seed as food, because they just can't wait for the harvest. Why go hungry now to feast later? They have a short-term mentality, but they won't be satisfied eating only seeds. People do that with their finances. They never share anything with others. They hold tight to everything they earn and spend it all on their own immediate needs. It's the old Scrooge mentality. They keep it for themselves thinking they will derive the most value from it that way, but the real value is in releasing it to meet another person's need. To prosperous people, seed is essentially an investment. They wouldn't hear of keeping it to themselves. They know the power their seed has to generate a hundredfold return.

Everything you do is an investment — every negative act, every harsh word, everything you say or don't say, affects the seed you plant. Some seed is good only for reproducing more seed, rather than consuming. Your investment today guarantees your future. By investing you show you have conquered fear and mastered procrastination and so guaranteed a harvest after a season of waiting. Let me ask you a question: does a wise farmer sow his *best* seed or his *worst* seed? A corn grower, for example, has to eat, like the rest of us, and he would be stupid not to eat his own corn. But corn growers have to decide what corn to keep as seed for their next crop and what corn to consume. My dad grew tomatoes and other vegetables in his backyard. He was a generous man and he used to give a lot of it away. When I was a boy, I would get so annoyed with him. I once said to him, 'Dad, why do you give the best stuff away to the neighbours?'

'They don't actually get the best stuff, son,' he replied. 'I divide my produce in half and the best goes back into the ground.'

A wise farmer chooses to plant his best seed because he wants to see the best harvest next season. He is thinking long term, prepared to make a sacrifice now to get a better return later. In the same way, prosperous people sow their best seed. It's simple: if you take away any of these elements from the process — seed, time, return — you won't get a harvest in your life.

A harvest takes time

Notice it's called the Law of Seed*time* and Harvest; *time* is important here. We cannot expect a harvest immediately. It takes time and nurturing and watering for the seed to take root and to grow, but once it has matured it will bear fruit in your life and in the lives of others. Harvests are seasonal, which means they always come around, guaranteed, because seeds are designed to grow and bear fruit over time. The same principle applies to your finances. Often the difference between your investment and your return on investment is time. You can't skip any step in this process: *investment* over *time* brings a *return*. In the same way, *seed* over *time* brings a *harvest*. It's the same process. Some people want it to be *investment* brings *immediate return*. Then again, some people want it to be even simpler: they just want a return — no investment and no time factor!

The Law of Seedtime and Harvest is probably the most powerful law in the universe. If you get it right, it affects everything you do. It affects life and it affects nature. It's really very simple. We all want a return. We all want results. The problem is that many of us don't want to take the action—make the investment—required to generate the results. We want a harvest, but are we prepared to do what it takes to ensure a harvest?

A harvest requires action

The miracle of the Law of Seedtime and Harvest requires action. A farmer can't stand in his field and say, 'Come on, give me crops!' He has to invest in that field through work. That's the only way this law will work for you. The bridge between today and your harvest is action. People ask me, 'Well how long should I keep investing?'

My response is always: 'Until...just until!'

'Until when?' they ask.

'I don't know.' You have to find out your own *until*—everyone's is different. Yours might be 'Until I make a million-dollar net profit'. Someone else's might be 'Until the grandchildren are all financially secure and have their own homes'. What's your *until*? You have got to invest in it.

> You have to find out your own *until*—everyone's is different.

In his *Art of Exceptional Living* CD series, Jim Rohn said, 'Your income rarely exceeds your personal development.' If you want your business to grow...if you want to increase your profits...if you want to increase your market share...if you want to increase your edge over your competitors...if you want to increase your customer loyalty...if you want to increase your profitability—it's got to come out of you in the form of investment.

Every investment costs something

When you love someone, is it an investment that costs you? Yes it is, because that love includes the potential for pain and heartache. The investment of trust can backfire too, as can our investment in a decision. There can be negative as well as positive returns on your investments. But if you live in fear of the negative returns, you will never have the experience that others dream of. If you never make the investment, you will never know the return.

About 15 years ago I spoke at a large network marketing convention. When my session ended I was handed an honorarium of $2500 and left the event to drive to my local church, where I had been asked to jump up on the stage towards the end of the service to say hi to everyone. As I was driving to the church I felt the $2500 cheque in my jacket pocket and a voice inside me said, *When you get to church, put that money into the offering bucket.*

Now, I had just given $40 000 to a community project earlier that week, so my immediate response was, *You have got to be kidding me! I've done my giving for the week. That $2500 is all I've got right now!* But the voice inside me responded, *It's all you'll have for a very long time if you don't give it away! Tonight, when you get up and speak to everyone, hand over that cheque.*

I got to the church about 30 minutes late, and as soon as I walked into the building one of the ushers grabbed me. 'Quick!' he said. 'We've been waiting for you. The senior pastor wants you to get up and do the collection before he gives his sermon.' (This meant inviting the congregation to donate to the ministry of the church.) *Man, that's not fair!* I thought. *I'm being set up here! How can I possibly* not *give the cheque if I'm asking everyone else to give!*

When I walked up onto the platform, I was still resisting, but as I was speaking I heard the same voice say to me, *If you let go of what's in your hand, He'll let go of what's in His hand.* Then the ushers began distributing the offering buckets. Everything was going well, until suddenly one of the ushers had the audacity to come up onto the stage and hand me a bucket as well—in front of the whole congregation! I looked down at my $2500 cheque for the last time. A song popped into my head: 'Goodnight sweetheart, well it's time to go...' Time seemed to stand still as I watched, for what seemed like an eternity, that piece of paper fall gently into the bucket.

A couple of weeks later I was speaking at a church in Atlanta, Georgia — on the other side of the globe. After the service the pastor asked me strange question.

'Pat, how much money do you need to live on each month?'

'I don't know,' I replied.

'Well I think I should give you $2500...' he told me. And I suddenly realised that the Law of Seedtime and Harvest had just kicked in. I was almost going to say, 'I knew you were going to give me that amount,' but then he added, '...every month for 24 months!'

My first thought was, *Wow! Next time I hope I receive a $50 000 cheque to give away!* But here's my point: if I had not made that $2500 investment, I would never have received that level of return. If we don't make the investment, we won't get the return. We have to take action for this law to become effective in our life. Simple as that.

Remember my story at the beginning of this chapter? If those generous business owners who provided new clothes and beds and a new bus for the rehab centre had not invested in those young men, we would not have seen such a dramatic change in their lives. The boys responded to those investments. They grew taller and stronger on the inside.

Every investment brings a return.

Different seeds bear different harvests

Different types of seeds will yield different types of harvests, and in the same way different types of investments will bring different types of returns. You can't plant watermelon seeds and expect a crop of bananas. So be intentional about what seeds you plant. The investment of words yields a harvest of feeling; the investment of conversation brings understanding; the investment of listening yields knowledge; the investment of knowledge yields change; the investment of *investment* gives you a return.

It's not just the *type* of investment that affects your return, it's also the *quality* of your investment. The quality of the seed you sow determines the quality of the harvest you reap. Do you want more quality friends? Then plant seeds of quality in the people you mix with. Do you want a quality relationship with your husband or wife? Then plant seeds of quality in them. Those secondhand beds, sheets, clothes and shoes donated to the rehab centre represented second-rate seed, so the return on that investment would have been second rate, but I wanted the boys in that program to get a first-rate return, so I had to orchestrate a first-rate investment. All good seeds will eventually bear good fruit.

Have you ever noticed that when it comes to giving, there are people who gladly part with old clothes that they've rarely worn (the ones that are outdated and should be thrown out anyway), but the newer, more fashionable clothes stay in their wardrobe? I don't get it! If *you* don't want to wear them, why do you think *someone else* will want to? If you think your old clothes are ugly, then guess what? They probably *are* ugly, and the chances are the recipient of those old clothes will think they're ugly too. Your attitude to giving will affect the quality of your return. If you want a better quality of life, you have to invest a better quality of seed.

> Generosity breeds abundance. If you want money, then be generous with your money.

Generosity breeds abundance

I have learned that if you want a life of abundance and prosperity, you have to be generous — not just charitable, but generous. Generosity breeds abundance. If you want money, then be generous with your money. If you want abundance, then be abundant in your giving.

A young boy was sitting on the kerb watching the world go by when he saw a bright red Ferrari coming up the street. The Ferrari pulled up and a man stepped out. He was dressed in a suit, his black hair slicked back and shiny. The boy walked up to him and said, 'Wow, you must be so rich!'

The man looked down at the boy and replied, 'I'm not *really* rich. I just turned 40 and my brother bought me this car as a birthday present.'

The boy looked back at the Ferrari and with a faraway look in his eyes he declared, 'I wish...I wish I could be a brother like that!'

Most people want to be the one receiving gifts, but there is so much more reward in giving! This young boy wanted to be the giver. Who do you want to be? The person needing a million dollars or the person giving a million dollars? Be generous. Be a giver. And watch what happens to your finances, your relationships, your career and your business. But make sure you are intentional in your generosity. Don't give just because it makes you feel good or because you feel guilty. Wealthy people give expecting a return, so why shouldn't you? I am always looking for opportunities to be generous, but the truth is I am always doing it for me. I always ask the question, *What's in it for me?* That's what prosperous people ask themselves before they give. Don't put good money into a bad organisation, because both they and you will end up broke.

I know you are probably shaking your head right now and saying, 'You are giving with the wrong motive, Pat!' No I'm not! We should always expect an outcome from our seed. A farmer would be a fool to plant some seeds in the ground and then think, *Oh well, I'm not really expecting much!* Some people think, *I just give from the goodness of my heart.* Well, that's just foolish! You *should* expect a return from your gift.

Investment is the act of using something you already have to get something you want.

Whatever I want in life, I have to give it away first

I remember one day speaking off the back of a truck in a black neighbourhood in Toledo, Ohio. It was one of the poorest communities I have ever been in. Graffiti covered the walls. Car bodies with no doors and wheels lined the streets. I stood up on that truck and surveyed my surroundings. I noticed a group of young guys playing basketball across the street. To try to draw a crowd, we set up barbecues and began giving out hot meals and food parcels. It didn't take long for a small crowd to form. So I started to speak. A group of homeboys stopped to listen. The basketball players came across to see what was going on.

I spoke about dreams. I challenged them to look beyond their circumstances to what they could achieve if they used what little they had. I talked about the Law of Seedtime and Harvest. When I had finished speaking, a large black lady approached me with a dollar bill in her hand. Hanging onto her were several young children dressed in ragged old clothes.

'Preacher man,' she hollered (I was a minister at the time), 'I want to give you a donation.'

I hesitated, because I didn't want to take her dollar bill. 'But ma'am...' I started to say.

'Wait a minute,' she cut in. 'I know what you're going to say. You and your fancy clothes. You don't need my dollar bill, is that right? Well I know you don't need my dollar. But I've learned something: whatever I want in life, I have to give it away first. So you better take my dollar, because if you don't take it, I won't be getting anything back!'

So I took that dollar bill. I have to tell you it was one of the hardest things I have ever had to do. Later that day I found out that she was a single mother with five kids. A few weeks later I received a letter from her with a photo enclosed. 'Preacher man,' she wrote, 'got myself a new job at the hospital, got myself some nice clothes, and got the kids a picture for their wall.' The photo showed her kids wearing brand-new clothes.

Every year she sent me a letter and a photo of her and the kids. And every year she would tell me about how she had just been promoted and was earning more money. The second year she was managing a few staff. The third year she was running a whole department. By the fourth year she wrote to tell me about her $150 000 job in charge of a hospital wing and how a man had come into her life. She said, 'I gave you a dollar, and I got myself a future, got myself a man…'.

Back then we had set up in my office what my staff and I called the 'Wall of Heroes'. On that wall I had placed a photo of this woman with her five children taken that first year I met her. She was one of our heroes. She knew the power of a generous spirit. She understood and applied the Law of Seedtime and Harvest.

That law can transform your life. It's one of the greatest principles of all. It's timeless and transcends every culture and every age. Your investment is the only control you have over your future. You cannot control the seasons and you have limited control over other people. But you *can* control your investment, and that will determine your return. There are some things in life you can't change, but the one thing you *can* change is your investment. Trust the process of the Law of Seedtime and Harvest, for over time it *will* return to you a harvest.

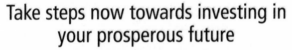

Take steps now towards investing in your prosperous future

Determine now that you will become a giver. Don't be held back by what you think you don't have. Everyone has something they can give. And don't be held back by those around you who urge you not to be generous.

Write down what you have that you can give this month to someone or some cause. It may be $10. It may be your time. That's your seed. Then beside each seed, write down *who* or *what* you want to give it to. Last, write down *why* you want to give that seed to that person or cause or organisation. It's your *why* that will drive you.

Seed no. 1:

_____

Seed no. 2:

_____

Seed no. 3:

_____

Chapter 8

What are you thinking?
Unleash your mind to unleash your wealth

Janite Lee, a 52-year-old Korean-American, ran a wig shop in downtown St Louis. One Saturday morning in early February 1993, her cousin drove her to the Route 3 Gift Shop and Lottery in Sauget to buy only her second ticket for the Illinois Lottery. The next day she learned she had won $18 million. What a windfall!

Janite took her winnings in 20 annual installments of $620 000 after taxes. She soon bought a house for $1.2 million. Some years later she sold the rights to the winnings for an undisclosed lump sum. She began by donating to the political campaigns of well-known politicians, including President Bill Clinton. Janite had a reading room at Washington University's law school named after her. In 1997 she was ranked 31st on a list of the top soft money donors to the Democratic National Committee. That put her a notch below the Boeing Company. The following year she was ranked in the top three of individual political donors in Missouri for the year.

But then her financial world began to unravel. Among the bad investments she made was a Bombay Bicycle Club restaurant. Reports indicate that gambling and credit card debt also ate away at her fortune. In one year alone she lost nearly $347 000 at several casinos in the St Louis area. That same year, 2001, she missed a few bank loan payments and car payments. In July of that year she filed for Chapter 7 bankruptcy. According to the court filing, she had $700 left in two bank accounts and no cash on hand.

Her generosity to a variety of political, educational and community causes was commendable, but how can someone lose $18 million in eight years? A long-time friend tried to explain the loss: 'As you know, anyone who wins the lottery, everyone comes to them.' That's true, but there was a deeper issue.

Janite Lee was not alone. Not by a long shot. Many other winners of million-dollar lotteries have lost it all — people like Jeffrey Dampier of Florida, Barry Shell of Ontario, Evelyn Adams of New Jersey, Fred Topous Jr of Michigan, William 'Bud' Post of Pennsylvania, Willie Hurt of Michigan, Juan Rodriguez of New York City, Suzanne Mullins of Virginia . . . the tragic list could fill this page and more. And the sad truth is that many of us are in the same boat as these lottery winners who lost it all. What is it that causes us to spend more than we earn or own? What causes us to behave irrationally when it comes to money? What is it inside so many of us that sabotages our journey towards prosperity?

What did your parents teach you about money?

I have known too many people who have reached a certain level of wealth and then slid back into the red. One year they are driving a brand-new Mercedes and have enrolled their children in a private school, the next year the Mercedes is for sale and the children are back in the public school system. *Why does this keep happening to me?* they wonder. A few years ago I was talking with a salesman in New Zealand who had been struggling to consistently maintain a high level of success. While we were sitting chatting in a café, he said to me, 'Pat, I don't know what it is about my life, but it seems every time I hit a certain income level, I start to feel guilty and I self-sabotage my higher earning capacity. I always slip back down to my original income. I am sick and tired of the rollercoaster ride. How can I stop this from happening?'

'What did your parents teach you about money?' I asked him.

'Oh, my parents taught me nothing about money,' he told me.

A few minutes later, when a BMW 7 Series drove past the café, the salesman recalled, 'When someone drove past in an expensive car in our town my dad used to say, "Look at that man. He must be a thief or a con man."'

As we continued to talk, he told me this story: 'Back in the 1970s my uncle was earning $60 000 a year selling exterior cladding for homes. My parents often talked about him. Apparently his mother would say to him, "$60 000 a year is too much money! That's greedy!"'

'You told me your parents didn't teach you anything about money!' I reminded him.

'They didn't.'

'Oh yes they did! They taught you that if you earn more than $60 000 a year you're greedy. They taught you that if you own an expensive car you're a thief or a con man. They taught you that if you're earning more than the average person, then you must be doing something wrong.'

Like so many of us, this salesman had a mindset problem that had been embedded since his youth. It was this mindset about money that had been limiting his prosperity. I have found that a mindset can be like a virus. It can remain hidden and dormant inside you for a long time. Often you don't even know it's there, but while you go about your daily life this mindset holds you back and you wonder what's wrong with you.

Your mindsets control your behaviours

Once people believed that the Earth was flat and that if you sailed across the ocean you would fall off the edge. Even after the great voyages of explorers such as Christopher Columbus and Ferdinand Magellan, the flat world theory persisted among many people, limiting their understanding of the world. That's what I mean by mindset control.

A mindset is an inherent belief that controls your behaviours. A belief is not an idea you possess, it's an idea that possesses you. It's a very powerful influence on your life. Your mindset about money controls how much money you make and keep. Your mindset about relationships controls how successful you are in your relationships.

What has shaped your beliefs about money? If your mindset is that money is always incredibly hard to come by, or that wealth is somehow inherently wrong, then before you can truly prosper you will need to change this way of thinking. In chapter 10 I develop this concept further.

Wealthy people have fewer mindset problems about money than others. You need to change your mindset about money to consistently think the way wealthy people think. We all need the right kind of mindset to achieve wealth and prosperity. The simple but powerful truth is that by changing your mindset you'll change your destiny. The bottom line is that your income won't keep you where your mindset can't hold you. You can't have a million-dollar income with a five-dollar mindset. Every one of those million-dollar lottery winners who lost it all had a mindset that could not sustain their new level of wealth.

> Wealthy people have fewer mindset problems about money than others.

To show you what I mean by mindsets about money, here are 12 poverty mindsets and 12 wealth mindsets that I've spotted over the years. See if you can relate to any of them:

12 mind viruses about money

- *Poverty mindset:* I'll never be able to afford that!

  Wealth mindset: I'm going to work out how to afford it!

- *Poverty mindset:* I'm not made of money!

  Wealth mindset: I'm made up of belief systems and thought patterns that determine my wealth.

- *Poverty mindset:* I didn't have it easy as a kid, so why should I make it easier for my kids?

  Wealth mindset: To achieve my success, my kids have had to make sacrifices, so they should be rewarded.

- *Poverty mindset:* No-one ever gave me a free lunch!

  Wealth mindset: I'm going to be the person who buys the lunch.

- *Poverty mindset:* Money made him greedy!

  Wealth mindset: No it didn't—money magnified what he already was!

- *Poverty mindset:* The rich keep all the secrets to themselves!

  Wealth mindset: I'm determined to learn from those wealthy people who share their knowledge in seminars and books.

- *Poverty mindset:* No-one in our family ever amounted to much!

  Wealth mindset: I'm not going to let my family history hold me back.

(*continued*)

12 mind viruses about money (*cont'd*)

- *Poverty mindset:* Money is the root of all evil!

  Wealth mindset: It's the love of money—not money itself—that is the root of all evil!

- *Poverty mindset:* I could never wear that! I could never drive that! I could never live there!

  Wealth mindset: I'm going to try on that dress, test drive that car and walk through that house, because I have the capacity to one day own it.

- *Poverty mindset:* Money won't make you happy!

  Wealth mindset: Well, neither will poverty!

- *Poverty mindset:* I wonder how many people he had to walk over to get to where he is!

  Wealth mindset: In getting to where he is, I wonder how many people he helped.

- *Poverty mindset:* I don't have what it takes!

  Wealth mindset: I can learn what it takes.

Your thoughts determine your life

Your outward behaviour will always conform to your internal mindset. This means that if you want to change how you behave outwardly, you first have to change how you think. Even if you think you want to be wealthy, you will never achieve wealth if you are governed by thoughts of lack. To bring about change in your external world, you have to work on your mind, your attitudes and your belief systems. Put simply, your thoughts determine your life. The input of your thoughts determines the output of your actions.

Let me show you how it works: first, you need to be aware of *how* you think and *why* you think the way you do. Once

Pathway to Prosperity

you've developed an awareness of the way you think, you are then in a position to change. If you change your thinking, it will change how you feel. If you change your feelings, it will change how you act. If you change your actions, it will change your level of prosperity.

It's a five-stage process that looks like this:

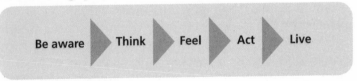

Be aware ▶ Think ▶ Feel ▶ Act ▶ Live

If you can become aware of how and why you think a certain way, you can end up changing the way you live, whether it's in the area of your finances, your relationships, your career or your business. Unfortunately, the process does not work in reverse. Some people want to change the way they live without first changing the way they think. It simply doesn't work that way.

This process explains why your thoughts determine your life. People try to change their life without changing their thinking. Instead of wishing your *life* was better, start wishing *you* were better. You are the sum total of where your thoughts have brought you to this point. So if you want to advance financially, you've got to think differently from now on. Your mindset sets the course of your life. That's why two people can be brought up under the same circumstances, with the same parents and the same influences, and yet one succeeds financially and the other doesn't.

> Your mindset sets the course of your life.

Much of your success will be the result of having the right mindset. One person looks at a mountain and declares, 'That's too big to climb!' Another person, facing the same challenge, thinks, well, the mountain can't get any bigger but my spirit and my ability can. 'I'm bigger than that mountain!' Prosperous people don't look at challenges in the same way others look at them. They look at challenges with a solutions mindset.

Have you listened to the news lately? The unemployment rate is rising. The cost of food and fuel is constantly increasing. More and more businesses are facing bankruptcy. The national debt is spiraling out of control. The media feed us with a constant barrage of negativity. 'Oh, it's tough out there!' they tell us over and over. When the media inform us that we're facing 6 per cent unemployment, how do you respond? It's easy to get sucked into the poverty mindset of shock and dismay, but a prosperous mindset immediately thinks, *Well that's great news, because it means 94 per cent of people are still working!*

How do you see yourself?

How do you look at challenges? What images dominate your life? You and I will always move towards the predominant images in our mind. You'll have heard the ancient proverb, 'As a man thinks in his heart, so is he.' If you see yourself as a victim of other people's decisions or of the environment you are in, then that's what you will always be — a victim. If you're going to prosper in life, you have to stop spending all your energy looking for something or someone to blame. Instead, focus on the solution to your challenge — your mindset.

An old Cherokee Indian once told his grandson about the struggle that takes place in our heads. 'There is a battle going on between two "wolves" inside us all,' he told the boy. 'One wolf represents evil. It is full of negativity such as anger, envy, jealousy, sorrow, regret, greed, arrogance, self-pity, guilt, resentment, inferiority and ego. This wolf always tries to get us to do what we should not do. The other wolf represents good. It is full of joy, peace, love, hope, serenity, humility, kindness, benevolence, empathy, generosity and compassion.'

The grandson thought about it for a minute and then asked his grandfather, 'Which wolf wins?'

The old man replied, 'The one you feed the most.'

If you feed your prosperity mindset more than your poverty mindset, that's what is going to win in your life. If you see yourself as a successful property developer, then feed that mindset as much as you can so it grows. If you constantly see yourself as not having enough time, that will become a reality for you. Just don't feed that image any more. Starve your thought processes of that image, and don't keep telling everyone you don't have enough time.

Choose faith over fear

Fear and faith are always competing for space in our minds. Fear and faith are two sides of the same coin. They are both belief systems. If you believe 'I don't have time' or 'I'm too busy', then those fears will eat away at your soul and you will have no time for those activities that will bring you wealth.

Fear and faith are two sides of the same coin.

Some of us focus on the fear of losing money. If that's you, then let me tell you this: everyone I know who has made money has also lost money. So get over that fear, because it will only hold you back from prosperity. You're going to lose money eventually…just be careful not to lose it all.

If you believe your fears, then that's what will come true for you. Have you ever feared something bad would happen to you and when it finally happened you declared, 'I knew that would happen!'? You proved that that's where your fear was. On the other hand, if you believe in positive things, then that's what will come true for you. For many of us, our fears are preventing prosperity from becoming a constant reality in our lives. You can never be prosperous if the images that govern your life and actions are dominated by fear, lack and negativity. If these images plague your mind, then they are going to dominate your reality.

Are you ready for a mind shift — to get rid of thought patterns, ideas and mindsets about money and wealth that have kept you contained? Are you willing to kick out those mindsets that have prevented you from stepping into the truly prosperous life that you were born for and that is waiting to be discovered? Are you ready to start thinking like a millionaire?

Characteristics of a wealthy mindset

Here are a few characteristics of a wealthy mindset. The list is not exhaustive, but it will help you begin to understand what kind of thinking it takes to become a candidate for a life of continually increasing prosperity.

- *Play to win.* Having a wealthy mindset means that you play to win as opposed to simply playing not to lose. At half-time in the 2005 soccer final of the European Champions League, AC Milan had a 3–0 lead over Liverpool. Then, in the second half, Liverpool scored three goals in six minutes — and they went on to win the final in a penalty shootout. AC Milan went from playing to win to playing to defend their 3–0 lead, and ended up losing the match. A person with a prosperity mindset always stays on the front foot, pushing forward, no matter how far in front they imagine they might be. This type of mindset plays to advance and to win, not merely to maintain a level or a lead.

- *Constantly ask questions.* A person with a prosperity mindset constantly asks questions and searches for answers. Unlike the person with a poverty mindset, they don't assume that they already know it all. They are inquisitive and not merely opinionated. Rather than being an armchair expert, a prosperity thinker is always learning something new. When in conversation with someone who knows more than they do about something, they don't pretend they know more than they do. Instead, they adopt a learning attitude and defer to the superior knowledge of the other person. They see it as an opportunity to expand their own understanding.

- *Ignore criticism.* The prosperity mindset is able to ignore criticism. A person with a prosperity mindset does not listen to the critics, but instead listens to mentors and leaders. Successful people tend to be criticised more than anyone else, so to be successful you need to be able to ignore your critics.

- *Be committed.* A person with a prosperity mindset goes beyond desire to commitment. It's not enough just to want to be prosperous — you have to be passionately committed to becoming prosperous. Life follows our convictions and our focus, not our desires. Desire is a starting point, but as long as a thing remains only in the realm of desire, it is only an option. At the drug and alcohol rehab centre I met many young men who desired to break their addiction, but unless they were prepared to be totally committed to changing, their desire was not enough to get them there. When we move from the realm of desire to the realm of commitment, what had been optional becomes non-negotiable.

- *Develop self-worth before net worth.* People with a prosperity mindset have a different understanding of their personal worth. They develop self-worth before they develop their net worth. You can be paid either for your time or for the value you bring to people. A poverty mindset sees time as the primary basis for payment — you work a certain number of hours and get paid on an hourly basis. This means your level of prosperity is determined by your hourly rate and the time you are able to give to your work. A person with a wealthy mindset understands that time is irrelevant to prosperity and that wealth is much more about whom they are and what they do than it is about how many hours they work.

- *Learn from mentors.* To have a prosperity mindset is to recognise the need for mentors, people you can look up to and from whom you can seek guidance and inspiration. These are people who have been successful and have achieved things you are still aspiring to achieve.

- *Use what's in your hand to achieve what's in your heart.* People with a prosperity mindset use what is in their hand to do what is in their heart. People with a poverty mindset are not driven by what's in their heart and, as a result, their hands are tied. People like Bob Geldof and U2 lead singer Bono are passionate about causes such as the elimination of poverty in the world. They have used their celebrity status as rock stars to try to influence world leaders to bring about change. 'Celebrity is ridiculous,' Bono once said. 'It's silly, but it's a kind of currency, and you have to spend it wisely.' He has been using what's in his hand to do what's in his heart. Start by asking yourself what's in your heart. What's your dream? What's your passion? Then ask yourself, *What do I have in my hand today that I can utilise to start moving in the direction of what's in my heart?*

- *Invest in experiences.* A person with a prosperity mindset uses money to buy outcomes and memories, not just material possessions. A person with a poverty mindset uses money simply to buy 'things'. Have you heard someone say something like this: 'Why would anyone want to spend $5000 on a five-day holiday? Once it's over, you've got nothing to show for it. If I had $5000 I'd buy a new plasma television!' This reflects a poverty mindset that sees money purely as something to be used to buy stuff. A prosperous person also spends money to enhance relationships, to have new experiences, to buy life-enhancing memories and to make life better for other people.

- *Value your seed.* As discussed in chapter 7, a prosperity mindset recognises the importance of the seed, whereas a person with a poverty mindset is concerned only with the fruit. Everything in life starts as a seed. Something that might look small and insignificant today could change the world tomorrow. Napoleon Hill, author of the seminal book *Think and Grow Rich*, once said, 'The world is full of unfortunate souls who didn't hear opportunity knock at the door because they were down at the convenience store buying lottery tickets.' Such people are trying to generate fruit in their lives without an understanding that fruit is the end result of a process that begins with the planting of a seed. So when a seed of opportunity presents itself, they fail to see its potential. A person with a wealthy mindset lives with an awareness that every day of our lives could be a day of opportunity, a day in which there is a seed to be seized and planted. Sometimes the seed is easily missed because seeds by their nature are very small. A giant oak tree grows from a tiny acorn. All the potential greatness of the oak tree lies in that acorn. If the acorn is never planted, the tree will never grow. A prosperity mindset always looks for acorns, not oak trees. Is your focus on the size of the tree or on the seed from which the tree grows?

- *Be courageous*. Another important characteristic of a prosperity mindset is courage. In his book *The Millionaire Mind*, Thomas J. Stanley identifies the courage to take financial risks as something most self-made millionaires have in common. Stanley argues that taking risks does not mean gambling. In fact, very few millionaires gamble at all. Here are a few wealthy mindset principles about courage and risk-taking that were revealed by a group of millionaires whom Stanley surveyed:

  - When it comes to mindset think success — don't veer towards failure. Ask yourself what the possible positive outcomes are, then move towards that goal.

  - Be a believer in yourself and be committed to hard work. These are two surefire ways to break down your fear and anxiety.

  - To build a bigger you, prepare and plan for success. Be organised and focus on major issues.

  - Get involved in physical exercise. It develops mental toughness, discipline and energy.

  - Almost 40 per cent of all millionaires have strong spiritual faith. A strong faith gives you a higher propensity to make sound financial decisions.

Understand that while your mindset won't change in a day, it can change daily. It will take effort and consistency over time, but the rewards will be amazing. Author William Arthur Ward once said, 'Nothing limits achievement like small thinking, and nothing expands possibilities like unleashed imagination.' The only limitations on your mind are the ones you put on yourself. Unleash your mind and you'll unleash your wealth!

Take steps now to unleash your mind and unleash your wealth

Here are four steps you can take to develop a prosperity mindset:

1 *Renew* your mind. Be proactive in depositing new positive thoughts in your mind every day.

2 *Replace* old mindsets. If the mindset you have today isn't going to get you to where you want to go in life, get a new one. Trade in your old mindset for a prosperity mindset. Even the most positive thoughts you have will be short-lived if you hold on to negative mindsets. If you don't actually change your old thinking habits or patterns, then the positive thoughts will soon be overpowered. You have to consciously get rid of old mindsets, then start to replace them with new patterns of thinking. Begin seeing the world around you as being full of opportunity rather than impossibility.

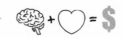

3   *Realign* your thinking by regularly asking yourself,
    Is this the right way to think? Become a little
    introspective. Think about your thinking. When you
    find yourself acting in a way that is not conducive
    to increasing your prosperity, ask yourself, *Why am I
    acting like this? What mindset is causing me to behave
    in this way? How should I be thinking with a wealthy
    mindset? What needs to change?*

4   *Re-establish* your convictions. Some things in life
    are a matter of preference, but others are a matter
    of conviction. A preference is usually something we
    can take up or leave behind, but convictions are not
    negotiable. A conviction is not a thought you possess,
    it is a thought that possesses you. Convictions are the
    things for which people are prepared to make great
    sacrifices. Some people even die for their convictions.
    What convictions drive you? Are your convictions
    propelling you forward into a life of success and
    wealth? Is prosperity a preference for you or a
    conviction? Is prosperity non-negotiable in your life?

\$\$\$\$

Chapter 9

Who are your friends?
Your friends influence your wealth

Several years ago, when I was running the drug rehab centre in Sydney, a political friend, Alan Cadman, introduced me to the then Prime Minister of Australia, John Howard. I'll never forget the day Alan told me he had arranged for me to meet him. I admit I was very nervous about it, knowing I would feel totally out of my comfort zone. I even told friends I didn't want to go, but he insisted, so I went along.

On the day, I was waiting in a room for the PM's arrival, when the door opened and in walked Alan along with the leader of our nation. They walked straight up to me and Alan said, 'Prime Minister, this is my friend Pat Mesiti.'

Mr Howard reached out and grabbed my hand. 'Young man, nice to meet you,' he said. 'You're the one helping young men who are addicted to drugs.'

'Yes, sir,' I replied.

'I hear you haven't come to us to ask for any government funding,' he continued.

'No, sir. I'm a capitalist. God gave me a brain and access to people. I don't want government funding because then your department would try to tell me how to run my rehab centre.'

'Oh, I like you!' he replied with a big smile.

At that moment Alan turned to the prime minister and said, 'Sir, if Pat ever calls you...if he ever needs some help, would you take his call as a favour to me?'

'Absolutely!' the prime minister responded.

I walked out of that room with my head held high and my spirit soaring.

I am so thankful for friends like Alan Cadman. Good friends change your life. They connect you. They inspire you. They lift you up and promote you. We cannot build wealth without them.

Friends help us build wealth

A while ago someone I know lost $27 million. At that point it would have been so easy for him to go off and hide, to shut himself away from his friends. Instead, he went looking for them. He said, 'I don't know how I'm going to do this, but I just know I need to be around the right people at this time. I need to plug into the right friends.' Last year he made a net profit of $2.5 million. He is on his way once again to a very prosperous future. He was connected and that made all the difference.

The great English poet John Donne once wrote, 'No man is an island.' We need friends to help us achieve our dreams. While most of us don't have direct access to politicians, prime ministers or presidents, there are others who can show us a roadmap to get us from where we are today to where we want to be in the future. After all, many of them have been where you and I want to go, and the best people to guide us are those who personally know the way.

Who are these people? Well, if your dream is to build a large corporation, there are many corporate leaders who can give you direction. They can show you the route they took when building their business. They can show you their map. If your dream is to have enough money to retire at age 40, then there are countless men and women who built fortunes before they turned 40. They can point you to paths they took that you too could follow. If your dream is simply to get out of debt, there are people in your circle of influence who have already put their financial house in order. They too will have a map that they can share with you to show you how they got there.

Many of these people began where you are now, and I have no doubt that in their time they were willing to admit they needed help. People with a prosperous mindset are willing to concede what they don't know, to acknowledge when they are lost. These types of people are humble enough to seek out the guidance of people who do know. Prosperous people aren't wealthy because they knew everything they needed to know. They are wealthy because they were willing to ask for directions from others and to follow the pathways travelled by other prosperous people.

Don't be sucked in by the herd assumption

If until now you have been following the wrong crowd, then perhaps you have been sucked in by what Andy Stanley calls the *herd assumption*. As he explains in his book *The Principle of the Path*, the herd assumption kicks in when we assume that since everyone we know is doing something a particular way, it must be the right way. 'If everybody you know is mortgaged to the hilt, driving two leased vehicles, and applying for a home equity line of credit, then it can't be all that bad. The problem, of course, is that everybody is headed for a similar destination at which no one has yet arrived.'

But just because everyone around you is doing it, it doesn't mean it's the right thing to do. Don't blindly take financial advice from people who have never been where you want to go. Don't listen to well-meaning relatives and friends unless you aspire to end up like them. Some of them may be just as lost as you, so it would be foolish to take financial direction from them.

King Solomon, in the Book of Proverbs, repeatedly encouraged us to listen to wise advice:

'A wise man will hear and increase learning, and a man of understanding will attain wise counsel.'

'The way of a fool is right in his own eyes, but he who heeds counsel is wise.'

'By pride comes nothing but strife, but with the well-advised is wisdom.'

'Without counsel, plans go awry, but in the multitude of counselors they are established.'

Fools ignore wise advice and then wonder why they don't prosper.

By listening to the *right* people, the wise will prosper financially. Fools ignore wise advice and then wonder why they don't prosper. Why is it so difficult for us to ask for advice from people who have done what we would like to do? Don't let pride get in the way of your prosperity. Find someone who knows the way, ask them for their advice and then follow that advice. Asking for advice does not mean you lack wisdom — quite the opposite!

The American entertainer Will Rogers once said, 'A man only learns in two ways — one by reading, and the other by association with smarter people.' American author Christopher D. Furman writes, 'If you want to be a winner, hang around with winners.' If your friends aren't helping you reach your financial destination, go find some friends who will! If your friends aren't ahead of you on the pathway towards a prosperous future, then don't rely on their financial advice and don't follow their financial lead.

If your friends despise your prosperity, they're not your friends. Some people around you may say, 'Who do you think you are? You rose above the pack and all of a sudden you think you're better than us?' How sad! You've got to start associating with people who will cheer you on when you do well — people who want to pick your brain and ask, 'How did you do that? Teach me. I want to know.'

Friends feed either your strengths or your weaknesses

Some people are fearful of climbing to another level of financial increase because it could mean losing their current associations. Your friends will feed either your strengths or your weaknesses. Whoever cannot increase you will eventually deplete you. If your friendships are depleting your prosperity, you need to reconsider those associations because their mindsets will cripple you. You will never reach a prosperous future with friends who are not willing to travel the same road.

A prosperous mindset recognises that you will function according to the people with whom you surround yourself. Everyone is influenced, even financially, by the people around them. The truth is that your income will rise to the level of your friendships. Your friends affect your income and your expenses. If they are borrowing more than they can afford and spending more than they earn, that may influence your financial behaviour too. Their mindsets and their habits will probably rub off on you.

So who is influencing you in the area of your finances? I know you wouldn't let someone deliberately push you off course, but someone might gently nudge you off course little by little without you noticing it. A boat with a small hole in the hull can sink drop by drop. Allow positive influences from successful people to encourage and stretch a prosperous mindset.

Don't be shaken by the negative opinions of critics

Plenty of people will find reasons to dismiss your financial ambitions, but a prosperous mindset will not be shaken by the negative opinions of critics. For every major achievement in history, someone somewhere said it couldn't be done. Right now some people may be telling you:

'You don't have what it takes!'

'It has been tried before, so what makes you think you can succeed where others have failed?'

'You're being too ambitious!'

'That's too risky — just play it safe like other people.'

'Why do you want to be rich? Just be happy with what you have.'

> Rather than listening to the critics and sceptics, hang around the dreamers.

Rather than listening to the critics and sceptics, hang around the dreamers. I love being around people who dream. They encourage and inspire you when you need a boost. They keep you on your pathway to prosperity.

The eight types of friends who will help you succeed

There are eight types of friends we need in our lives. These are the people who most contribute to our success. See if you can recognise them in your own life. Remember, you won't necessarily be lucky enough to have all eight types in your life. You need only a few to help you along the way, but if you don't have any at all you will find yourself in trouble.

The builder

This type of person builds us up and pushes us towards our dream. A builder continually invests in our development and genuinely wants us to succeed, even if it means they have to go out on a limb for us. Builders are generous with their time as they help us recognise our strengths and encourage us to use them productively. When we want to do more of what we already do well, a builder is the one to go to. Like the best coaches and managers, these friends lead us to achieve more. If we need a catalyst for our financial or professional growth, then we should stay close to a builder.

We all have people in our lives who try to tear us down. That's life, and that's why it is important to be around people who motivate and inspire us. Just as a house builder sometimes has to tear down unnecessary walls and other structures in order to expand and improve the house, a friend builder will sometimes help us with a bit of internal demolition and renovation so we become better in certain areas of our lives such as our finances.

Do you have a builder in your life? It could be someone you have not even met face to face but who you listen to or watch on a regular basis. I have had some great builders in my life. For years American author and speaker Jim Rohn was one of them. I bought every one of his CDs and books. I'd listen to him while I was running, walking or driving. He taught me so many invaluable principles of life. He inspired me and built me up. I owe him a great debt of gratitude!

The champion

Who is championing your cause? Who sticks up for you and tells everyone else how great you are? We all need a champion behind us. Over the years I have had a number of champions. These are people who like you so much they love telling others about you, sometimes without your even knowing. As with all good champions, you can't create them. They just turn up in your life. They are a rare breed and you need to cherish them, because with just a few whispered words in the right ears they can increase your capacity for wealth and prosperity.

The companion

This is someone you do life with, someone you can rely on and lean on. A companion is always there for you, no matter what the situation. When something big — good or bad — happens in your life, this is one of the first people you call.

Sometimes a companion will sense your thoughts, feelings and actions before you know them yourself. Companions are loyal and take pride in your relationship. A companion is a friend who will make huge sacrifices for you and the first person you would call if something goes wrong.

The connector or bridge builder

This is the person who introduces you to others, who opens doors for you, who widens your network and makes your business bigger. Connectors know an endless variety of people. Friends who play the role of connector are always inviting you to lunch, dinner, drinks or other functions so you can meet new people. This pushes you outside your current network and gives you access to potential new friends.

Who is the person who brings key people into your world, who connects the dots in your life? If your connector knows you need a better accountant, she will arrange for you to meet an accountant she knows. If he knows you are interested in getting into the share market, he will introduce you to a friend who has made a lot of money in shares. Connectors can save you a lot of time, effort, money, energy and pain simply by building bridges between people. They love doing it and your life will be blessed if you have one or two connectors as friends.

The energiser

Energisers are your fun friends who are always ready to give you a much-needed boost. You have more positive moments when you are with these friends. They are quick to pick you up when you are down. They can make a bad day good and a good day great. They are always saying and doing things that make you feel better.

Energisers have an amazing ability to figure out what gets you going. When you're around these friends, you relax, smile and laugh a lot more. Some of us are way too serious. It does us good to laugh at ourselves sometimes. If you want to chill out and have a good time, call your energiser.

So who is the energiser in your circle of friends? We all want to build wealth for our future, but are you enjoying your *now*? Make sure you have a friend who energises your now.

The mind opener

Who is the one who opens your mind to new experiences, such as a new style of clothes, different types of food, new travel destinations, new books or new hobbies? Make sure you have a friend who broadens your experience.

I'll never forget the first time I bought a very expensive tie. Back in those days I thought $80 was a lot of money for a tie. I was shopping with a friend when I saw a stunning tie on a rack and thought, *Wow, I want that one!* Then I checked the price tag and quickly moved on to a cheaper one. My good friend — my *mind opener* — noticed what I had done and stopped me.

'Pat, what are you doing?' he challenged me.

'I'm buying this tie,' I replied.

'But you like that one over there better, don't you?' he said.

'I do, but it's $15 more.'

'On the economic scale of the rest of your life, that's really not much money!' he responded. 'Come up a level, Pat. Why not buy both ties?'

So I did. My friend stretched me to think bigger. He did it then and he has done it to me many times since. I am a better person for it. I'll always remember that experience, though.

You see, my friend drew me out of my comfort zone and taught me a valuable lesson. I am so thankful for friends who prod me and challenge my mindsets. (If you think an $80 tie is too expensive, then perhaps today you need a friend who is a mind opener in your life.)

The navigator

Navigators are the friends whose advice keeps us headed in the right direction. We go to them when we need guidance, and they talk through the pros and cons with us until we find an answer. In a difficult situation, they help us identify a positive future and keep things grounded in reality.

Any time you are at a crossroads and need help making a decision, you can always look to a navigator for help. They are the ideal friends to share your goals and dreams with, and when you do, you'll continue to learn and grow. When you ask a navigator for direction, they will help you reach your destination. Sometimes we need people who know us well enough and are honest enough to tell us, 'No, don't do that. Do this instead. Try this option.'

Who are the navigators who keep you on track?

The collaborator

A collaborator is a friend with similar interests — the basis for many great friendships. You might share a passion for sports, hobbies, religion, work, politics, food or shopping. When you talk with a collaborator you are on common ground, and this can serve as the foundation for a lasting relationship. Through those conversations you often discover that you have similar ambitions in life.

We all need someone who shares our interests, joys, passions and dreams, and who works with us on these. Collaboration equals multiplication. On your own you can reach a certain level of achievement, but when you work alongside someone else you can achieve so much more. Find people you can collaborate with on projects.

Look for friends who will lift you higher

With these eight types of friends in your own life, you will experience life to the fullest. They will enhance your journey towards a prosperous future. Oprah Winfrey once said, 'Surround yourself with only people who are going to lift you higher.' She's right. If you want to move beyond where you are now, look for these friends.

If you already have these wonderful people around you, do they know the valuable role they play in your life? Have you shown them gratitude? Please don't take them for granted. Constantly appreciate them and get closer to them. Tell them, 'Thank you for being my champion/collaborator/ energiser...'. Regularly acknowledge their contribution to your life.

Do to others as you would have them do to you

But don't wait for these friends to turn up in your life. Go out and be one or more of these types of friends to others around you. Can you be the energiser for someone else? Can you be a connector for a friend? Can you be the builder for someone? Go up to them and say, 'Let me help you do that. Let me teach you how to do it.' Find these people in your world and lift them higher.

Perhaps in your heart you know you have got to do something about your friendships. You know you have to take action. You know you want more than what you are getting right now. Don't jump straight into excuses about why you can't find the right friends. Find out why you *can*. With good friends, your life, your income, your finances and your relationships will be so much more enriched.

Take steps now to find the right friends

If you don't have these friends in your life, you will have to find them sooner rather than later. Sometimes they are so obvious you don't even notice them, so you may not need to look far to find them. Write down the names of friends who currently fill these roles in your life.

Then write down the names of friends who could potentially fit these roles in the future, and determine to nurture those friendships. Invest in them, not for selfish gain, but with the goal of contributing to their lives too.

Current builder: _____

Possible future builder: _____

Current champion: _____

Possible future champion: _____

Current companion: _____

Possible future companion: _____

Current connector: _____

Possible future connector: _____

Current energiser: _____

Possible future energiser: _____

Current mind opener: _____

Possible future mind opener: _____

Current navigator: _____

Possible future navigator: _____

Current collaborator: _____

Possible future collaborator: _____

$$$$

Chapter 10

What's your (money) story?

The powerful truth about your relationship with money

Once Mandy had rarely taken her credit card out of her purse — in fact, she used it only for emergency expenses. But gradually she began to use the card whenever she felt like rewarding herself with something new. Soon she had acquired a second card, then a third, and before long she had five cards. Each month she paid the minimum amount on each card. It wasn't long before her debt cycle kept her awake at night. It sapped all her energy and began to affect her health. One day Mandy went to a debt counsellor and began following her advice. The program set out for her helped her pay off almost all her credit card debt. But just as she was about to become totally debt free she relapsed into her old ways. Within months she was back to five credit cards and a new mountain of debt.

For Mandy, being out of debt had been a new and unfamiliar experience. It was as if she needed the challenge of a huge debt to provide a focus or a reason for feeling bad, a feeling she had grown accustomed to. Becoming debt free was like stepping into unfamiliar territory, and this generated its own stress and anxiety. So she reverted to her five-card debt to get back into her familiar comfort zone.

Sadly, Mandy's story is shared by millions around the world. We all have a money story. Most of us are not aware we have one but it's there nevertheless, deep within us. It shapes who we are and therefore drives our money decisions whether we know it or not, and whether we like it or not. If you can change your money story, you can change your life story. It's that powerful!

In his book *The Secret Language of Money*, David Krueger suggests that if money was just about mathematics, none of us would have any debt. Maths makes sense. We can understand it because there are formulas we can follow to get the results we want. But money is not just about numbers; it's also about feelings.

We give money its meaning

It's what we *do* with money that makes it complicated. We give money much more meaning than it deserves. We make it out to be much more than it really is. We make it much bigger than it is. We use money to do things it isn't designed to do. Life would be so simple if we could just earn, save and spend money. Instead we get all emotional about it. We crave it, promote it, steal it, love it, dream about it and use it to influence others. We live and breathe money. We earn it and then we spend it — it comes and it goes. It's a constant challenge for most of us. What we do with our money often seems to make no rational sense. We spend beyond our means. We argue, worry, sue, divorce and sometimes even die over money.

Max and Sophie wanted to build a backyard deck and gazebo. They estimated the project would cost them $5000, so they took out a home equity loan and found themselves a contractor. Within a month the contractor had been paid the full $5000 but he was only halfway through the job. When Max and Sophie reviewed it more carefully, they realised they would need another $6500 to complete the job. But here's the killer: they discovered that the project would add only another $4500 to the total value of their home. They didn't have the money to continue, so they decided to borrow it to complete the work. 'We *have* to finish this!' they reasoned. This is called 'throwing good money after bad'! This experience jeopardised their financial future, and they never fully recovered. Are elements of this story familiar to you?

Your relationship with money

The truth is your money problems have nothing to do with money itself and everything to do with your *relationship* with money. This relationship influences your financial success, along with everything else in your life. It determines how much you think you're worth.

In her book *The Money in You*, Julie Stav talks about money personalities. She argues that our personalities, our temperaments, our hopes, our fears and our self-esteem are all bound up in our relationship with money. Each one of us relates to money in a unique way. Our temperament influences us. Our personality traits determine our money decisions. Financial freedom is impossible to achieve, therefore, without first knowing something about our money personality.

> There is an inescapable connection between our feelings and our finances.

There is an inescapable connection between our feelings and our finances. Successful investors have learned to recognise and understand their money personalities and use this knowledge to their advantage. You too can find a permanent solution to your financial worries by discovering your personality strengths and weaknesses and understanding how they relate to your financial decisions. Try to work out which of the money personalities I list in the following pages best describes you.

The emotional spender

As soon as the emotional spender gets paid, she goes shopping. Shopping changes her mood. There is no logic in the way she handles her money, but there is certainly a lot of feeling. So if you are an emotional spender, there is an adjustment to be made if you want to build up your wealth.

The first step is to build into your money management an automatic trigger that diverts an amount of money into a savings or investment fund as soon as you get paid. In other words, save it before you spend it. Banks and other financial institutions have inbuilt systems that prevent emotional spenders from spending the money they have just earned. You simply need to schedule an automatic transfer to take place the same day you get paid every week, fortnight or month.

The emotional spender needs some motivation to help her manage her money. So determine that once you reach a certain level of savings, you will reward yourself with a vacation or a down payment on a new dress or a romantic five-course dinner. It's much more exciting to save when you know what you're saving for. The idea, says Julie Stav, is to reverse the old habit of *spend–pay–spend* with *save–spend–save*. She also warns us not to call it a budget! Instead, tell the emotional spender it's a spending plan.

The generous spender

This personality type has one overriding purpose in life: to serve others. He is generous with his time, expertise and contributions. He follows his heart, even in his purchasing and investment decisions. He is all heart and no head. The obvious danger here is that often his family suffers when he allocates so much of his time and money to others.

If that's you, then here's what should work for you: link your financial wellbeing with your family's happiness and your charitable projects. Socially responsible investing is tailor-made for this type of investor. Once you understand the concept of providing for yourself and your family first, you can afford to dedicate your time and energy to helping others. This makes it much easier to establish a savings and investment system.

The meticulous money manager

On the surface, the meticulous money manager is the perfect wealth creator. She loves budgets and deciphering the tax laws to take full advantage of any loopholes. She is a detailed perfectionist who finds it hard to make a decision, which means good financial decisions are often not acted on. She won't admit it, but she knows she needs to let her hair down and lighten up.

If that's you, here's what you need to do: set a time limit whenever you look into a financial project, and stick to it; and when considering all the risks from every possible angle, don't forget the risk of *not* making a decision.

The adventurous spender

The adventurous spender is rarely out of a job or out of ideas to make money. When hard times hit, his connections soon get him up and running again. He prides himself on making quick decisions based on gut instinct. He can see all possible angles to any problem and often finds creative solutions that no-one else has thought of. He is very comfortable working in unstructured environments with no rules or regulations.

Now, here is the downside:

- He is impulsive and adventurous in his purchases (often buying new styles of clothes, new genres of books and new types of music).

- His purchases are not necessarily expensive, but he does make a *lot* of them.

- He has no budget to follow and believes that saving money is boring and unnecessary.

- He uses credit cards a lot and is likely to be in debt.

- His motto is 'You can't take it with you'.

- He strongly believes that purchase decisions should be made based on gut instinct.

If you are an adventurous spender, here's what you can do to manage your debt better and increase your savings. First, if you have a lot of credit card debt, transfer the balance of the card with the highest interest to the one with the lowest interest. This will mean more of your payment goes towards reducing your debt and will reduce the number of payments you need to make each month.

Second, the *envelope system* may suit your personality, especially if you are never quite sure where your money goes each month. Make a list of each monthly expense and designate an envelope for each one. Include an envelope with your name on it as well; this is your personal savings envelope. Try to place about 10 per cent of your income in this envelope each month. The envelope system suits someone who hates poring over a budget.

The squirreling Scrooge

This money personality has very little debt and no extravagant expenses, and is very tight with her money. She thinks:

- she will quickly lose all her hard-earned money if she is not careful

- she must hold on to all her money now because it's likely she won't have much in the future

- it's better to be safe now than sorry later.

However, here's where she fails in the area of money: she is terrified about her financial future. She is a Scrooge and doesn't enjoy life to the full. There is a real danger that her saving and investment methodology will leave her with much less than she anticipates when she retires. This type of money personality needs to learn how to spend less time worrying about money and more time enjoying quality of life with her family and loved ones.

The prosperous personality

So what do the millionaires of this world do? The wealthy don't fall into any one money personality but they still manage to accumulate wealth. Here's their secret: they recognise their strengths and weaknesses and use their strengths to propel them to success. In *The Money in You*, Julie Stav describes the keys to wealth that prosperous people adopt along their pathway:

- They believe in the value of investing; they typically invest between 15 and 20 per cent of their household income every year.

- They know how to find ways to turn talents and passions into money.

- They associate with people who have a similar passion and focus to make money.

- Along with a positive attitude, they see opportunities to learn and grow.

- They know the steps they have to take to achieve wealth, and they recognise that their course of action is a work in progress that requires persistence and resolve.

- They are confident in their ability to make money.

- They are very motivated to earn money. They genuinely feel good about money and feel justified in their use of money.

Your money story

A key ingredient of financial success is the ability to recognise your own money story and tweak it or rewrite it to get you on the pathway to prosperity. David Krueger sees our money problems as tied to our *money story*—the story we try to tell with our money, the way in which we use money to shape the world around us, and how that world then affects our life.

Did you know that you have a money language? Like any language, you learned it while you were young, mainly through the words, actions and attitudes of your parents. Watching your parents' money behaviours and listening to them talk about money formed a language pattern for you to learn from. Subconsciously you connected the dots and established assumptions about money based on those observations in your youth. After all, that's how we form most of our assumptions, attitudes and mindsets, and we do this without being consciously aware of it.

Let me give you some examples of the behaviours you may have observed in your parents. When they discussed financial matters, were they happy or sad? Did they smile or frown? Did they agree or argue? Did they speak confidently and purposefully or anxiously and timidly? What behaviour and language did they adopt when they talked about your pocket money, music lessons, toy purchases or college tuition? Whatever you observed provided nonverbal cues that influenced your secret money language.

If you are a parent today, be aware of the money language you are passing on to your own kids. They will automatically adopt a money language based on your behaviour and what they hear in your words and tone of voice.

Your money story forms your identity

Your money language makes up your money story. Your money language is like the building blocks that form, support and colour your story. We all have a personal story that makes up who we are. Our story shapes our identity and our assumptions about the world around us. We understand ourselves and others through stories. For instance, when we observe people sitting in first class in an airplane, what judgements do we make about them? Do we see their privilege as a reward for their success or as a demonstration of their greed? The answer you give will depend on your own storyline.

What kind of story do you have about your own life? Do you see mostly difficulties and challenges along the pathway to your financial destination, or do you see rewards, achievements and accomplishments? Former president Harry Truman once said, 'A pessimist is one who makes difficulties of his opportunities and an optimist is one who makes opportunities of his difficulties.' A pessimist has a very different story from an optimist.

So what exactly is your money story? Well, according to David Krueger it is the subconscious story or narrative you constantly tell yourself about who you are, what money means to you and what it says about you. It's the story you tell yourself and others about how much you deserve, how much you're worth and how much you're capable of achieving. For example, when you see a new car and you decide to buy or lease it, you're probably acting out your money story. How? By subconsciously believing that this car will prove you are worth something. This new car will bring you self-esteem. Perhaps you feel it will make people respect you more. The purchase then validates you.

Here's another example: let's say that so far, despite your best intentions, you have struggled financially. Your attitude may be, *Well I haven't seen much money come my way yet, but I'm managing to make ends meet!* What you're most likely hearing is a constant inner voice whispering, *I'm never going to get out of credit card debt. I have no hope of achieving my dreams!* If that's the story you are always telling yourself, then that's the storyline your life will follow. David Krueger writes, 'Your life is the manifestation of your beliefs. Change begins when you recognise that the story you're living is the story you are writing.'

Circumstances challenge your money story

Whether you are an inherently positive or negative person, some things remain the same for all of us: the environment around us keeps changing. Events keep spiralling out of control. Almost nothing stays constant. Just as you are about to achieve a financial windfall, a contract falls through or is ripped up. Just as you are about to invest in some property, you lose your job or a major client. Sometimes, no matter what we do, circumstances seem to conspire to pull the rug from under our feet.

At times you may feel like you have no control over your financial situation. Perhaps you feel that your financial circumstances have been predetermined and that one crisis after another has thrown your financial life into chaos. If you feel that way, remember that your story is a work in progress. It is constantly developing. The good news is that you can pick yourself up off the canvas and rewrite your story at any point.

Nelson Mandela rewrote his story. How would he have felt spending 27 years in a South African prison? His story — from promising lawyer to resistance leader to prison lifer — went through dramatic changes. But through incredible patience and grace, he took control of his story. Today we remember his great successes. The world is full of people who have transformed their stories after bad starts. People like Elvis Presley, Oprah Winfrey, Bill Clinton, J.K. Rowling and Barack Obama were born into one story only to create a new one. According to *Forbes* magazine, almost two-thirds of the world's billionaires built their fortunes from scratch. They started off at the bottom and worked their way to the top. J.K. Rowling was a single mother on welfare when she began writing the Harry Potter series. As she developed her plot she rewrote her own financial story, and in the process she came to be the first person in history to become a billionaire by writing books.

You can pick yourself up off the canvas and rewrite your story at any point.

You are the author of your own story

No matter how much of a financial mess you may be in right now, there is one role that you will play every day of your life: you are the author of your own story. You dictate your story. No matter how your circumstances have affected you in the past, you are still in control of your destiny. As the author of your story, you can rewrite it and edit it.

Your parents, friends or spouse may have been telling you for years that you can't become wealthy. Perhaps you have repeatedly told yourself that you have no capacity for wealth. If you believe it, then that's the money story that will come true for you. But what would happen if they told you that you *can* build a wealthy future? And what if *you* told yourself you can? Then you would be rewriting your money story.

Your money story affects everything in your life, including what you eat, drink, read, dream about, plan and buy. That's why it's so important that you understand it and get it right. But the first step is to recognise and understand it. You see, the greater part of your money story remains hidden, and for the rest of your life it will direct your future wealth—until you discover it, examine it and change it.

The four layers of your money story

The only way we can change our money story is to examine it by peeling back the layers. Addicts know that to manage their addictions they have to treat them seriously, to face them and the damage they cause. We have to treat our money story in the same way.

David Krueger identifies four distinct layers to a money story. The first layer is our feelings. We make money decisions based on our underlying feelings. This gives money its emotional meaning to us, and over time these meanings morph into our beliefs about money. Within each of us, money can stir up deep feelings such as jealousy, fear, resentment, pride and compassion. Feelings are the deepest layer of our money story and form the core of our story.

The second layer is our behaviours — the things we do for money. Our behaviours can reveal to ourselves and to others our secret money story. It's not what we say we believe or what we think we believe that gives it away. It's what we actually do that most clearly expresses what we really believe. For example, when we choose to upgrade a car, quit a job without an obvious reason or shop beyond our means, our behaviour provides the best window into our world and reveals the truth about what money really means to us.

The third layer of our money story is our thoughts — how and what we *think* about money. We tend to buy emotionally and then justify our actions rationally. Very few of us do it the other way around, so in most of us our rational mind kicks in after we have made a financial decision. Thoughts are what we *tell* ourselves the story means and not necessarily what it *really* means. Just as an 'official' history of events is often shaped and interpreted according to the author's perspective, the story we tell ourselves is often a misrepresented version of what really happened. Sadly, this rational explanation often drives the real story underground.

The fourth layer of our money story is our experiences. Our reactions and responses to money help form our story and at the same time reveal much about our story. We all have unique experiences with money, and these become the substance of our money story.

The beliefs that form your story

Let's examine the subconscious assumptions and beliefs that form your story. It will take courage and willpower to explore the root feelings behind the things you do with money. But let's have a go. Let's go back to your youth, where your money story began. What themes or messages did you pick up from your parents, grandparents or guardians? Are some of the following themes or messages familiar?

'No-one can have lots of money and be genuinely happy as well.'

'If it was good enough for us, it's good enough for you.'

'Don't make more money than you actually need for you and your family; anything more and you're just greedy.'

'Money corrupts us and ruins relationships.'

In *The Secret Language of Money*, David Krueger suggests you ask yourself the following questions to learn something about your money story:

Regarding your past...

What experiences, attitudes and ideas about money can you remember picking up in childhood?

How did your parents feel about and behave with money?

How did they feel, talk about and behave towards those who had more money than they did?

Regarding your present...

What do you now believe about money? For example:

- People who have a lot of money are lucky.

- People acquire money when and if they deserve it.

- Wealth and spirituality are mutually exclusive—you're either rich or good, but never both.

What do you use money to express or do?

- As a reward for obedience or performance?

- To enhance your personal and professional growth?

- To create opportunities?

Regarding your future...

> How fully, honestly and regularly do you speak
> with your spouse or partner about money, finances,
> spending, goals, savings and debt?

> How open with your children are you about
> money details?

> What do you tell your children about money?

> And how consistent is this with how they see you
> behave towards money?

There are so many money stories that prevent us from reaching our desired financial goals. One such money story that is prevalent in our culture is that the most successful people are workaholics who sacrifice family and fun to achieve their success. We think of Ebenezer Scrooge in Charles Dickens' classic novel A *Christmas Carol*. This unattractive character taught generations of potentially wealthy people the money story that you cannot have both money and a happy life. In the same novel, Dickens introduced the impoverished but happy Cratchit family. This story does not need to be true for you and me. We *can* enjoy success *as well as* happiness.

So what is your current money story? I challenge you to search deep within yourself to find the money story that lurks in your psyche like a virus affecting your financial health. What makes your money story so powerful is that it usually remains undetected and unexamined. But not for you, because you are about to unlock the riches you have desired for so long simply by discovering and rewriting your own money story.

Take steps now to discover and change your money story

To help you get to the bottom of your money story, write down your answers to the following statements and questions:

1   To me, money means *(answer with a single word)*

    _____

2   What were your most recent purchases of more than $100?

    a   _____

    b   _____

    c   _____

3   What did each purchase mean to you? How did each purchase make you feel?

    a   _____

    b   _____

    c   _____

4   If they didn't give you that feeling, would you have still bought them at that price? *(Yes/No)*

5   My life is a *(tragedy, comedy, drama, adventure and so on)*

    _____

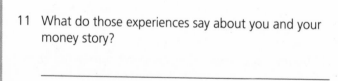

6 In my life story, I play the *(choose a word or phrase to describe your role)*

_____

7 What is the greatest annual income I can reasonably expect to earn?

$_____

8 What is the greatest annual income my money story will allow me to earn?

$_____

9 What have been the three most significant experiences with money in your life?

a _____

b _____

c _____

10 What feelings made each one so significant?

a _____

b _____

c _____

11 What do those experiences say about you and your money story?

_____

_____

$$$$

Chapter 11

Are you learning your way to wealth?

Feed your mind to feed your wealth

When I was at school I had a teacher who enjoyed trying to scare the life out of me. She would notice me daydreaming and sneak up behind me and scream at the top of her voice, 'Mesiti, pay attention!' That always got my attention! I hated school, not just because of this teacher. It didn't help that my Italian mother was always so protective of me. As I was leaving for school each morning, she would yell, 'Pasquale, watch out when you cross the road! If you get hit by a truck, don't you come crying to me!'

One of my worst subjects was maths. For one maths exam I got 0.7 out of 100, and that 0.7 was for spelling my name correctly. I improved slightly after that, with some unexpected help. I was the vice-captain of the school rugby league team, and my failing maths had become a real problem for my coach. He pulled me aside one day and said, 'Son, I have been the head of the sports department for over 20 years. In that time we have never been able to reach the inter-schools rugby league finals. This year we have a shot at the title. Now, according to the school rules, if you don't pass maths I can't put you in the team, and I need you in the team. So listen up. I am going to give you the answers to your next maths exam.' So when the next test came along, thanks to my coach I achieved my all-time maths test record of 27 per cent! I was so proud of myself.

Obviously arithmetic was not my strong point, but thankfully an academic education has little to do with financial success later in life. If we are honest with ourselves, many of us didn't much enjoy listening to our teachers, watching them scratch out chalk lessons on a blackboard, and having to do homework when we could have been playing outside. We'll even admit that we've forgotten most of what we were taught at school anyway. I have to agree with Albert Einstein: 'Education is what remains after one has forgotten what one has learned in school.'

Your pathway to a prosperous future requires constant learning throughout the journey.

Failing in maths didn't stop me from achieving wealth. Perhaps you bombed out at school too, but it's never too late to learn. Higher education guru Anthony J. D'Angelo says, 'The only real failure in life is one not learned from.' He also advises, 'Develop a passion for learning. If you do, you will never cease to grow.' Your pathway to a prosperous future requires constant learning throughout the journey.

The school I learned most from was the School of Hard Knocks. If you look back over your own life, you'll discover that you learned many important lessons through adversity and challenge. Benjamin Franklin wrote, 'Those things that hurt instruct.' And boy, was he right! Marriages start because of love but continue because of commitment. Businesses start because of opportunity, but they continue to succeed because of drive, vision, and the birth of new ideas and concepts.

Your prosperity depends on personal development

Most people want the results of prosperity without the commitment to prosperity, but prosperity requires personal development. When I was 18, I made it a goal to feed my mind by reading and listening to personal development material every day. Whenever I opened my mouth, I wanted to have something to say that would have a positive impact on the people around me.

If you want what you've never had, you must be committed to doing what you've never done before. People yearn for a change of lifestyle without a change of thinking. They want everything around them to be better, but they themselves don't want to become better. Your growth is a process, not an event. It is a daily thing you do. What you do daily will determine what you are permanently.

To develop a prosperous future, you've got to do what prosperous people do, read what they read, go where they go, attend the events and seminars they attend. I've discovered that sometimes those who most need to grow and feed their minds are the least likely to do so. What a tragedy that they are too lazy or too comfortable to grow! Education is not expensive, but ignorance is! Carl Rogers said, 'The only person who is educated is the one who has learned how to learn and change.' Unfortunately, some people are committed to staying the same. As a result, they always get what they have always got.

Grow a bigger you and you will grow a bigger income

Prosperous people do habitually what a broke person does rarely: they invest in personal development. If you grow a bigger you, you grow a bigger world and a bigger income. But it all starts with personal development. Just as your body can't function on a steady diet of junk food, your mind can't feed itself on a diet of TV shows, tabloid newspapers and gossip magazines. You have to get out of your comfort zone to get into the prosperity zone. If you commit to feeding your mind the right food, you will grow your value to others around you. And as your value grows, so will your wealth. As Benjamin Franklin also said, 'Empty the coins in your purse into your mind and your mind will fill your purse with coins.'

The greatest investment in your wealth is *you*. Unfortunately, far too many of us pay little attention to personal development. We invest in our health, our finances and our relationships, but we don't invest in our minds. When it comes to our education, there are three types of people. First, there is the naive person who says, 'One person can teach me everything.' Then there is the arrogant person who says, 'No-one can teach me anything.' Third, there is the prosperous person who says, '*Someone* can teach me what I need to know to earn more.'

> The greatest investment in your wealth is *you*.

Prosperous people look for successful people to act as their mentors. *Rich Dad Poor Dad* author Robert Kiyosaki said, 'If you want to go somewhere, it is best to find someone who has already been there.' Sometimes you will not be able to meet your mentor face to face, but you can usually access their books or audio teaching resources. In life you will learn from your mistakes or from your mentors. Take it from me, it's much easier to learn from your mentors.

A few years ago I was listening to an outstanding speaker at a business conference. I was totally captivated by the man's wisdom and insight and the angle from which he explained business principles. He was able to say so much in so few words. As I frantically took notes, it suddenly struck me that there was a resource table at the back of the room where the speaker's books and CDs were on sale. So I turned to one of my assistants and said, 'Quick! Here's my credit card. Beat the end-of-session rush and buy me one of everything on that table.'

The young man rushed away, but within minutes he was back with a frown on his face. He said, 'Pat, have you seen how many books and CDs he's selling?'

I told him to go straight back and do what I asked — buy everything. A few minutes later he came back again. This time he said, 'Pat, sorry to interrupt you, but I've calculated how much one of everything on that table is worth. There's about $7500 worth of material there.'

He still wasn't getting it. I was willing to invest any amount of money in having this speaker increase my wealth potential. So once more I said, 'Please, just go over there and buy everything that's on that table!' I went on taking notes, totally absorbed in everything this gifted, prosperous speaker was saying. But soon my assistant returned a third time with nothing in his hands. He whispered to me, 'Pat, I just want to ask you a question.' In a rather sombre tone he said, 'Is it worth it? It's going to cost you $7500!'

I looked him in the eyes and said, 'The clients I speak to are worth it. The readers of my books are worth it. When I give advice to people, they're worth it. And more importantly, my mind is worth it!'

Feed your mind to feed your wealth

Within five minutes he had bought that material for me, and within a couple of years I had turned that $7500 investment into half a million dollars. Is your investment in your personal development worth it? Do you value yourself enough to feed your mind? People want better homes, better cars, better watches and better holidays without becoming better people. Money isn't the issue—commitment to personal development is the issue. Show me a person who is committed to their personal development and I will show you a person who will add value to themselves, to their clients and to their businesses.

Educator and philosopher John Dewey wrote, 'Education is not preparation for life; education is life itself.' We learn most when we are most alive, when all our senses are heightened and challenged, when we learn concepts and skills outside the traditional educational environment. It's called experiential learning.

If you pause for a moment and think of some of the most significant, exciting and rewarding experiences in your life, usually they are the ones that turned on all of your senses — the buzz of a concert, the thrill of a large sporting event, the serenity of a five-course romantic dinner with a view of the sunset, the rush of wind in your hair as you glide over the ocean on a yacht. It's different for all of us, but when our whole body tingles, when we're really living out experiences that can change us forever, when we're immersed in an experiential environment that's feeding all our senses — that's a great investment of our money and time. That's when we really learn what life is all about, whether it has to do with business, family, relationships or wealth.

> You can *have* more simply by *becoming* more.

That's why I love live personal development events. And that's why you will love my wealth creation events (turn to the back of the book for a list of ongoing events). These events engage all your senses. You are surrounded by people brimming with positive energy, prosperity and success, sharing in their breakthroughs. That's where momentum builds momentum and, like the wind catching a sail, you suddenly find yourself racing down a pathway towards a life of wealth. When you attend my events, you will receive a complete toolkit to generate financial breakthroughs in your life. These events will:

- *Shift your mind.* You will learn to exercise the mindset of millionaires and look at the financial world from a totally different vantage point.

- *Touch your heart.* You will know how money changes lives for good in your family, in your neighbourhood and around the world.

- *Increase your wealth.* You will learn how to expand your current business or career, whether in property, finance, retail, insurance or network marketing.

- *Connect you with some extremely wealthy people.* You will be given opportunities to ask them about the roadmaps and pathways that led them to great wealth.

- *Place you on the pathway to a wonderfully prosperous future.*

The truth is that you can *have* more simply by *becoming* more... and you can become more than you are right now by investing in your personal development.

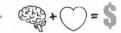

Take steps now to feed your mind to feed your wealth

The best way to achieve personal growth is to feed your mind through inspiring audio messages, video messages, books and events. There are numerous resources available to you, including those produced by the authors I have talked about in this book. You'll also achieve great results by investing in some of the other resources I have produced for you. You can find a complete list of all my books, audio messages and events on my website www.**mesiti**.com

Chapter 12

Afterword

Most of you will know the song, 'Somewhere Over the Rainbow'. It is one of my favourite songs. However, many of us live with the 'somewhere over the rainbow', and 'some day one day' mentality. Things are always going to come in the future, rather than acting now.

When I was working in drug rehabilitation I noticed young men would come in and say, 'One day I'm going to get my act together! Some day I'm going to stop doing drugs!'

When I entered the world of public speaking, I noticed that the 'some day one day' phenomenon is a deep-rooted problem and it manifests itself in various ways. You might hear someone say, 'Some day we are going to begin to put money away and some day we are going to really begin to take responsibility'. I often hear the some day one day syndrome from our politicians. They promise that some day one day all children in our nation will be free of poverty! I hear politicians say that some day one day, because of the policies we make today, our environment will be so much better! You know, they seem to place a long distance between the promise and the fulfilment. They put enough distance so that there's no accountability.

I often hear husbands say to their wives, 'Oh some day one day babe, we're really going to make it!' or 'We're going to buy that dream house some day one day!', that 'Some day one day I'm really going to stop my drinking' and that 'Some day one day…I will change'. Unfortunately, financial success does not work on the some day one day syndrome. Some day one day is hard to manage. It's obscure. It creates distance where there's seemingly no accountability, and there are actually no real steps to us achieving what we rightfully or actually deserve.

By overcoming the some day one day syndrome you will step over a threshold and into financial freedom. This is the one big step you must take.

Your financial progress is not linked to some day one day! It's linked to today, what you will do right now as we conclude this book with 12 steps to your prosperous financial future.

12 steps to your prosperous financial future

- **Step 1:** Recognise that your finances have become unmanageable and commit to change today, not in the future.

- **Step 2:** Prepare to do all that you can do to improve your financial position. What are you prepared to save today? What habit will you change today?

- **Step 3:** Ask someone else's advice to help restore your financial situation. Who is it that you will find today? What seminar can you attend today? What can you look up online or pursue from the pages of this book today? To be a student is to realise that you need someone else's wisdom and advice. You've already taken some action today — you've read this book! What advice did you glean from this book that you can implement today, not tomorrow?

- **Step 4:** Decide to turn your financial situation to someone who knows better, a professional or a friend who can give you good advice! The day you turn your life over to someone else, to give you advice, to keep you accountable, is the day you'll start to progress in life.

- **Step 5:** Make a fearless inventory of bad decisions you have made to this point. What's stopping you from doing that right now? Some of you may say, 'Well I'm finishing off reading this book!' Put it on pause, pick up a pen and begin to write down the mistakes you've made. Why? Because if you can see them, you're most likely not going to repeat them. Isn't it amazing that in life we often repeat the same mistakes over and over again?

- **Step 6:** Admit that on occasion you have taken steps down the wrong pathways of life. When will you honestly and truthfully admit this? It's different to step 5 because this is admitting that there are steps, steps that lead to your financial decision. What were the wrong steps you took? Now you have to trace them back!

- **Step 7:** Commit to learning all that you can. Remember that poverty is a result of misguided money! If you guide money correctly, it will lead you to prosperity.

- **Step 8:** Assess your friendships and commit to spend more time with people who have healthy financial habits. Every one of us in life must understand that our associations will equal our assimilations. Our friends today are affecting us financially. Their thinking is affecting you.

- **Step 9:** Be willing to remove the wrong money mindsets. What a step you can take today! Right now if you have wrong mindsets, write down the ones that you're willing to eradicate! Maybe right now one of the mindsets is, don't take action, procrastinate, and put it off tomorrow!

- **Step 10:** Make amends to anyone you have hurt financially with poor decisions. Right the wrongs you have made, and commit to a financial recovery.

- **Step 11:** Commit to renouncing your bad habits. Reject those habits and turn away from them permanently.

- **Step 12:** Get over some day one day syndrome! Commit to building wealth over the long term—this is not a get rich quick strategy. Assets are created and wealth is maintained over a period of time. The journey to financial prosperity is a marathon, not a sprint!

I wish you prosperity, abundance and success in all you do. I know if you follow these steps, and instructions in this book, your life can be financially free. I look forward to hearing about you, look forward to meeting you and look forward to seeing you.

'Some day' is always going to come but never does. The reason why some day never comes is because what you really have, is today. This is the day you must take a step in the right direction.

Yours in abundance.

Pat Mesiti

Other resources by Pat Mesiti

CD sets

The University of Success

Unleashing the Power of Prosperity

How to Stay Together Without Killing Each Other

Live at the Millionaires Club

What Makes the Great Great?

Living the Dream

Prosperity Accelerator

The Mind to Succeed

The Purpose of Prosperity

CD and book packs

Trilogy Pack

Massive Action Pack

The Ultimate Sales System Pack

Books

Staying Together Without Falling Apart

Men and women are different; we all know that. Most people are overworked, stressed-out and time poor. In our fast-paced society, men and women need new skills to enjoy successful relationships. This is a definitive guide to help men and women thrive together in modern relationships.

The $1 Million Reason to Change Your Mind

Change the way you think and you will change your world. This book teaches you how to shrug off the shackles of mediocrity, find your inner millionaire, and think differently about life and money...and get rich and happy along the way!

Soaring Higher

If you've looked adversity in the eye and wondered how you'll ever rise above it to see another sunny day, this book reaches through the storm clouds to lift you higher than you've ever been before. Pat shows you the view above your mountain and reveals simple steps to exploit your challenges and boost you above your circumstances. This book teaches you to soar!

Attitudes and Altitudes

Pat at his best! This book addresses the 'hows' of leadership. It deals with vital principles such as leader development, how to network and how to bring out the best in those around you. Pat speaks on growing big people, passion, leadership, mentoring, encouragement, attitude and credibility.

Dreamers Never Sleep

Pat, in his comical yet challenging way, will show you how to replace wrong perceptions with winning attitudes, deal positively with change, define your destiny, go beyond the 'norm', handle failure, and discover what success really is and how it can affect your world.

Opportunity Knocks

If you are one of those millions of people around the world waiting for an opportunity to take your life to another level, then this book is for you. Pat shows you how to recognise and grab opportunities that come your way, and to persevere with the opportunities you seize.

Wake Up and Dream

Discover the power of personal vision and how your dreams can help change the world. Pat's topics include rising above the limitations of your past, defining your dream, developing a plan to make your dream a reality, developing character, skills and attitudes that facilitate change, and unlocking the gifts and talents of those around you.

www.**mesiti**.com

Pat Mesiti's wealth creation events

Here is a list of some of the wealth creation events I run in Australia and Fiji. These events will fast-track your pathway towards a life of wealth. How? By surrounding you with people oozing positive energy, prosperity and success, by sharing with you the breakthroughs others are experiencing and by giving you a complete toolkit with which to generate financial breakthroughs in your life.

These events will:

- shift your mind
- touch your heart
- increase your wealth
- connect you with some extremely wealthy people
- place you on the right pathway to a wonderfully prosperous future.

La Dolce Vita (Gold Coast, Australia)

This all-inclusive experience includes a personal chauffeur from the airport, three nights' luxury accommodation, all meals, a three-hour drink package every evening, daily gifts, world-class speakers, exclusive nightly entertainment and much more!

Wealth Warrior (Fiji)

Travel to exotic Fiji to spend a week with some of the most successful entrepreneurs and leaders in their respective fields. This experience will transform your success and maximise your businesses potential.

Living the Dream Weekend (Gold Coast, Australia)

The Big Dream Weekend has changed the lives of all those that have attended, rekindled forgotten dreams and set untold participants on the path to their true destiny. Pat designed this seminar to stretch you beyond your current limitations and into the realm of your deepest desires—your true purpose and destiny.

Celebrity Evolution Experience (Sydney, Australia)

Develop the skills that will take you to new heights of success. Learn to speak with authority and power, capture an audience in 60 seconds, produce a best-selling book, package yourself, create a product that sells, manage the media, move people to action and close the sale.

You can find out more and register for any of these events on my website: www.**mesiti**.com.

P.A. Mesiti

MY SPECIAL REWARD TO YOU

For finishing this book, I would like to take you to the next level.
Get on board and become a part of my community!

Register online and start enjoying regular video insights that will help you fufill your financial, wealth and relationship dreams and goals!

This information is normally worth thousands of dollars, but by claiming your gift online it will be made available to you **ABSOLUTELY FREE!**

REGISTER TODAY
WWW.MESITI.COM/PROSPERITY
FOR MY
MOTIVATIONAL VIDEOS

SHIFT THIS

TOUCH THIS

GET THIS

...ALTH ACCELERATOR SUMMIT

COMPLIMENTARY DOUBLE PASS TICKET

*Think Differently About Life and Money –
and Get Rich and Happy Along The Way...*

...event details and to validate ticket call **+61 2 9999 6122** or email **events@mesiti.com**

This ticket is not redeemable for cash. Secure your seats and validate ticket prior to attending.

P.A. Mesiti

PRESENTS

LIVING THE DREAM WEEKEND

COMPLIMENTARY DOUBLE PASS TICKET

*Ignite Your Passion, Discover Your Dream, Turn On
Your Money Metabolism and Step Into Your Destiny...*

...event details and to validate ticket call **+61 2 9999 6122** or email **events@mesiti.com**

This ticket is not redeemable for cash. Secure your seats and validate ticket prior to attending.

P.A. Mesiti

PRESENTS

...UTRAGEOUS STREAMS OF INCOME

COMPLIMENTARY DOUBLE PASS TICKET

*Take Control of Your Financial Future –
And Start Living The Good Life...*

...event details and to validate ticket call **+61 2 9999 6122** or email **events@mesiti.com**

This ticket is not redeemable for cash. Secure your seats and validate ticket prior to attending.

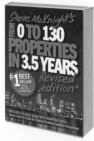